HOW CAPITALISM CREATES WEALTH & PROMOTES PROSPERITY

Antony P. Mueller

Copyright © 2018 by Antony P. Mueller. All Rights Reserved.

ISBN-10: 1731200676
ISBN-13: 978-1731200679

All rights reserved. No part of this book may be reproduced in any form or by any electronic or mechanical means including information storage and retrieval systems, without permission in writing from the author. The only exception is by a reviewer and by academics, who may quote short excerpts in a review.
Printed in the United States of America

based on "Beyond the State and Politics. Capitalism for the New Millennium"
First Printing: April 2018
Amazon KDP
New edition July 2018
ISBN-9781980571445
also available as e-book

CONTENTS

INTRODUCTION

I.   WHAT IS CAPITALISM AND HOW DOES IT WORK?
- *Capitalism in perspective* –
- *Backgrounder: Capital* –
- *Development stages of capitalism* –
- *Capitalism and the state* –
- *Backgrounder: Building blocks of modern capitalism* –
- *What are capitalists good for?* –
- *The stock market without puzzles* –
- *Commerce* –
- *Monetary economy* –
- *Equality is not justice* –
- *Origins of Western capitalism* –
- *Market process and competition* –
- *Backgrounder: Utility, value, and price* –
- *Prices and competition* –
- *Mass production* –
- *Freedom and capitalism* –
- *Summary*

II. THE POLITICS AND ECONOMICS OF WEALTH CREATION
- *The meaning of economic growth -*
- *Growth traps -*
- *Backgrounder: The rise and fall of parasitic economies -*
- *Economics of wealth creation -*
- *Backgrounder: time preference -*
- *Backgrounder: Interest, consumption, and savings -*
- *Value creation and capital structure -*
- *The state as an enemy of growth -*
- *Creative destruction -*
- *Obstacles to innovation -*
- *Free trade -*
- *Summary*

BIBLIOGRAPHIC REFERENCES

INTRODUCTION

While the 20th century experienced the transformation of manufacturing, technology is now revolutionizing the service sector. The professionals - ranging from medical doctors to lawyers, from educators to public administrators - will face tough challenges. The transformation is already on its way. Many apparently secure jobs will be wiped out. Robots and artificial intelligence make complex tasks not only cheaper but also perform better. The new technologies enter the consultants' offices, the legal chambers, the classrooms, and the hospitals. With a click, better diagnoses than humans could deliver show up on the screen in seconds - be it a medical assessment or the analysis of a legal problem. Machines are replacing even sophisticated occupations. What does the future hold for jobs, skills, and wages? What does this mean for the future of capitalism? What kind of economic system is best to meet the challenge?

In the 19th century, one could tell the farm boy to go to the city and learn a trade. In the 20th century, one could say to the young man or girl they should move ahead and go to study. These were all good pieces of advice. Yet in the new millennium, there is nowhere to go upward. The move from agriculture to industry, and from industry to the services, has ended. Now, to go to the university and to get a degree is no longer a guarantee for a well-paid and secure job. Professional positions fall victim to automatization and to the onslaught of artificial intelligence. The sprouts of the ladder are occupied. For one to go up, another one must come down. Upwardly mobile is a feat of the past.

What is the way out? The promise of 'jobs, jobs, jobs' will be in vain. The more the state tries to make jobs available and positions more secure, the more productivity declines, and incomes fall. The new millennium needs a different approach. The answer is to embrace fully technology. The more the new technologies become a complement to human work, productivity will rise. The urgency of having a fixed position as an employed person recedes. The use of one's car as a chauffeur for Uber and renting out one's house or apartment for travelers with Airbnb are examples of the things to come.

A necessary condition for the surge in productivity is less state and the end of politics. Less state and fewer politics would deliver the citizen from the heavy burden that now confronts him. Productivity would rise as the state fades away. The individual gets liberated from both sides. On the one hand, the burden of taxes and contributions falls. On the other hand, gains of productivity bring down the costs of living.

The current 'all-or-nothing'-trap ('either Yale or jail') would vanish. Now it is so that if one has a professional job, one's material situation is fine. Yet when one loses this position, the fall is enormous. We need a system that avoids this dichotomy. An anarcho-capitalist order would bring down the burden of taxes and of contributions. Free capitalism would open the path to vast productivity gains. Then, the urgency of having a permanent earning position would recede. One could live well even without having a secure job because productivity is so high that also temporary assignments offer a pay that is high enough to maintain a good life. The technology that takes away the jobs is the same that provides the tools which brings down the costs of living and makes leisure time attractive.

Nowadays, there are many professional couples who are both working because one needs two incomes to do well. Many would be glad to have only one breadwinner if they could maintain their living standard. Free capitalism would offer such chances because taxes and contributions would come down to a tenth of the present level and goods would cost less than half of their present prices with income several times higher than today.

Our present economic, political, and judicial system is ill-prepared for the challenge of the future. That was also the case over a hundred years ago at the beginning of the 20th century. Then, many wrong decisions were taken until a system took shape and became accepted that could accommodate the technological changes and the economic transformations. Yet now, new tribulations loom, and they make the dominant 'liberal' - social-democratic - system obsolete.

Resistance will arise - like that which came from the artisans and the home workers at the start of the industrial revolution. The workers feared that with introducing the new machines they would lose their economic existence and be condemned to poverty and misery. Yet they had no chance. And good for them - for because of the industrial revolution, the working class experienced a level of prosperity in the two centuries to come which was unimaginable at the time when the industrial revolution took off.

Protectionism, interventionism, imperialism, communism, and fascism were the many wrong answers in the past. Many believe now that the social-democratic version of capitalism would be the adequate system for the new millennium. Yet this not the case. It is no exaggeration to forecast that when we continue with the social-democratic way, the end would be state-bankruptcy. Serious analyses must conclude that the social security and welfare complex of healthcare, education, pensions, and social assistance have failed. The legal system is in shambles. Likewise, the expectation that the political management of the economy could guarantee employment, economic growth, and financial stability, is illusionary. Trying to maintain, to reform, and to expand the present system will lead to the opposite of the 'liberal' promises.

Without a change of the social security system, healthcare costs alone will absorb more than one fourth of the gross incomes. Pension provisions would require another fourth of the income. In a few decades, the ordinary taxpayer must confront obligatory contributions that exceed half of the income to pay for social security and welfare alone. Besides these contributions, the government would have to require another third of the incomes as taxes to finance defense and the other parts of the state apparatus. Such a burden is impossible to bear. Almost nothing would be left for private use. Before these projections can become a reality, the economy would break down. People would refuse to work, and businesses would stop to invest, the nation would become bankrupt.

Thus, the challenge remains: in the decades to come, young people can no more expect to have a high income just because they get a university diploma. Many job-secure careers in established professions will go away or experience profound transformations. The present horror of unemployment or of not finding the right job comes from being not able to bear the high costs of education, healthcare, housing, public security, and retirement without a high permanent income.

We need a new order. Repairs of the structures in place are not enough. Just as it had made no sense to improve the horse carriage to compete with the automobile, is it a futile effort to improve the current political system and to make the social security system more effective and the economy more efficient.

We need to make a turnaround. Instead of making the present system more social-democratic, we need a libertarian revolution. Instead of making capitalism more socialist, we need a more capitalist capitalism.

Free capitalism together with the drastic reduction of the state and the abolishment of politics would do away with the financial burdens that afflict the modern citizen. Not state intervention in economic life leads to prosperity. The path to affluence is the withdrawal of the state and the end of politics.

The new millennium will belong to those societies that discard the administrative state and move towards a capitalism that is free of the state and of politics.

A free economy in a free society requires three major institutional changes.

First, the selection of the society's representative body through a process of random selection;

second, a private monetary system to substitute the central banks;

third, the provision of law and security by private suppliers.

In order to establish a state-free society, insight must come first. The legitimacy of a free social order cannot come from the application of force - as it has been the case with all other political systems - but needs as its base the voluntary cooperation of the people to arise as a spontaneous order.

The tentative to establish an 'improved socialism', as it is the aim of the globalist scheme of a world government, would be even more deadly than the socialism of the 20th century. Yet also the milder forms of socialism and fascism, as they are practiced as interventionism, represent no valuable alternative. Likewise, it is pointless to expect that government could manage the economy and provide stability and economic growth so that everybody could have a well-paid secure job.

The more the state would retreat from private life, the less the burden of taxes would become. The present schemes of healthcare, education, pensions, legal services, housing, and welfare - not to speak of defense - are not only inefficient but also costly beyond needs. In these areas, the new technologies provide ample alternatives that would lower the costs while making the services better. Doing away with politics would eliminate the silly election campaigns. Sortition would stop the political culture of more government spending.

If we go on with the present system, the state will grow bigger and bigger. With the growing size of the state, governments will become more powerful. Without a halt, the present so-called 'liberal democracy' will transmute into a new totalitarianism.

The great debate is not only about jobs, but even more so how we can maintain human freedom in the face of the new technologies. In the new millennium, the demise of the state is a necessary condition for freedom. If we fail, humanity's fate is an age of slavery. If we succeed, we may welcome a new era of freedom and prosperity.

What we need is a new political and economic order, an order, which does not dilute capitalism with socialism, but a capitalism free of its socialist admixtures.

I.
WHAT IS CAPITALISM AND HOW DOES IT WORK?

Antony P. Mueller

"THAT MUCH MORE KNOWLEDGE OF FACTS ENTERS THE MARKET ECONOMY THAN ANY SINGLE PERSON OR ANY ORGANIZATION CAN KNOW, IS THE DECISIVE REASON THAT THE MARKET ECONOMY IS ABLE TO PERFORM BETTER THAN ANY OTHER FORM OF THE ECONOMY."
FRIEDRICH AUGUST VON HAYEK: "ECONOMY, SCIENCE AND POLITICS" - INAUGURAL LECTURE ON 18 JUNE 1962 AT THE ALBERT-LUDWIGS-UNIVERSITY OF FREIBURG I. B. (FREIBURGER STUDIEN, TÜBINGEN 1969, P. 11

- *Capitalism in perspective* -
- *Backgrounder: Capital* -
- *Development stages of capitalism* -
- *Capitalism and the state* –
- *Backgrounder: Building blocks of modern capitalism* -
- *What are capitalists good for?* –
- *The stock market without puzzles* –
- *Commerce* –
- *Monetary economy* –
- *Equality is not justice* –
- *Origins of Western capitalism* –
- *Market process and competition* –
- *Backgrounder: Utility, value, and price* –
- *Prices and competition* –
- *Mass production* –
- *Freedom and capitalism* –
- *Summary*

HOW CAPITALISM CREATES WEALTH & PROMOTES PROSPERITY

People are anti-capitalists not because of insight but out of ignorance. The term 'capitalism' emerged in the 19th century as a polemical concept. The negative connotations continue to stick until our time. Yet capitalism is as old as humanity itself if one understands capitalist production as the use of tools for manufacturing goods. At the turn of the 18th to the 19th century, modern capitalism arose as a system of production based on the private ownership of the means of production. The prominent feature of modern capitalism is that specialized firms operate with the goal of earning a profit. Since earning profits in competitive markets depends on productivity, the modern capitalist system compels the firms to maintain cost control and to strive for innovation.

Entrepreneurial competitive capitalism is an innovative economic system. Because productivity means wealth, capitalism is the economic system with the highest wealth creation. At all places where modern capitalism has taken hold, even in its diluted fashion, production and incomes have risen, particularly the earnings of the masses.

Modern capitalism as a monetary enterprise system distinguishes itself from the other economic forms of production by its feature to first ease and then abolish mass poverty. In capitalism, the customer and thus the end-user of the goods is the pivotal point of the system. In a market economy, the de facto owners of a business are not the legal owners in the formal sense. The customers of the firm determine whether the company can expand or must shut down. In a market economy, the economic owners of a business are its customers.

In a capitalist economy, not the state hierarchy determines the allocation of resources, but the preferences of the clients. The existential question of 'to be or not to be' in capitalism is 'to buy or not to buy' on the side of the customer which translates into profit or loss at the firm.

Different from socialism where the rule is to obey or to die, a capitalist economy is a consumer economy. Those companies, which resist the wishes of the consumers and pass them by, do not survive. The failed firms make way for those companies that meet the customer's requirements faster, better, and at a lower price. Competitive capitalism eliminates less productive companies and fosters the productive enterprises. This way, the overall productivity rises as the competitive process lifts incomes.

CAPITALISM IN PERSPECTIVE

'Capitalism' is a term that refers to a specific form of production that consists in the systematic use of capital and technology under the guidance of entrepreneurs. This system emerged around 1800 after a long period of incubation and has since then spread around the world. Capitalist production has led to a manifold increase in output per capita.

The final purpose of production is consumption. Production is the use of the factors of production – such as nature, labor, capital, technology, and entrepreneurship – to obtain the goods for human use. The pre-capitalist production process applied mainly nature and labor as the factors of production. The most primitive production process earns the fruits of nature without tools or with only a few instruments. Gaining one's living by nature and labor characterized the production process for most of history. Until the 19th century, slaves served as 'human machines'. The abolishment of slavery came with the industrial revolution. Machines substituted labor. This process has not yet ended. At first, machines substituted slaves, then the machines substituted most of the labor in agriculture. The 20th century saw the automation and robotization of manufacturing while the 21st century will experience the same in the service sector.

Only step by step did humans devise the systematic use of tools in production. Social cooperation and the division of labor has lifted output. But the increase of population and production went hand in hand. Nature worked as the limiting factor so that the production per capita did not rise throughout history until the capitalist revolution, which applied capital and technology to improve production in entrepreneurial firms.

Before the capitalist revolution - whose first manifestation was the industrial revolution – a group of people could improve its relative position concerning the access of consumption goods by extracting the goods and services from the labor force either of the subgroup within their own social body or by the conquest of an outside social group. The typical course of events was first to conquer and then to succumb the defeated people to slavery. A societal division occurred between the slaves and the ruling class with a small group of functionaries – such as the priests and the state officials - in between.

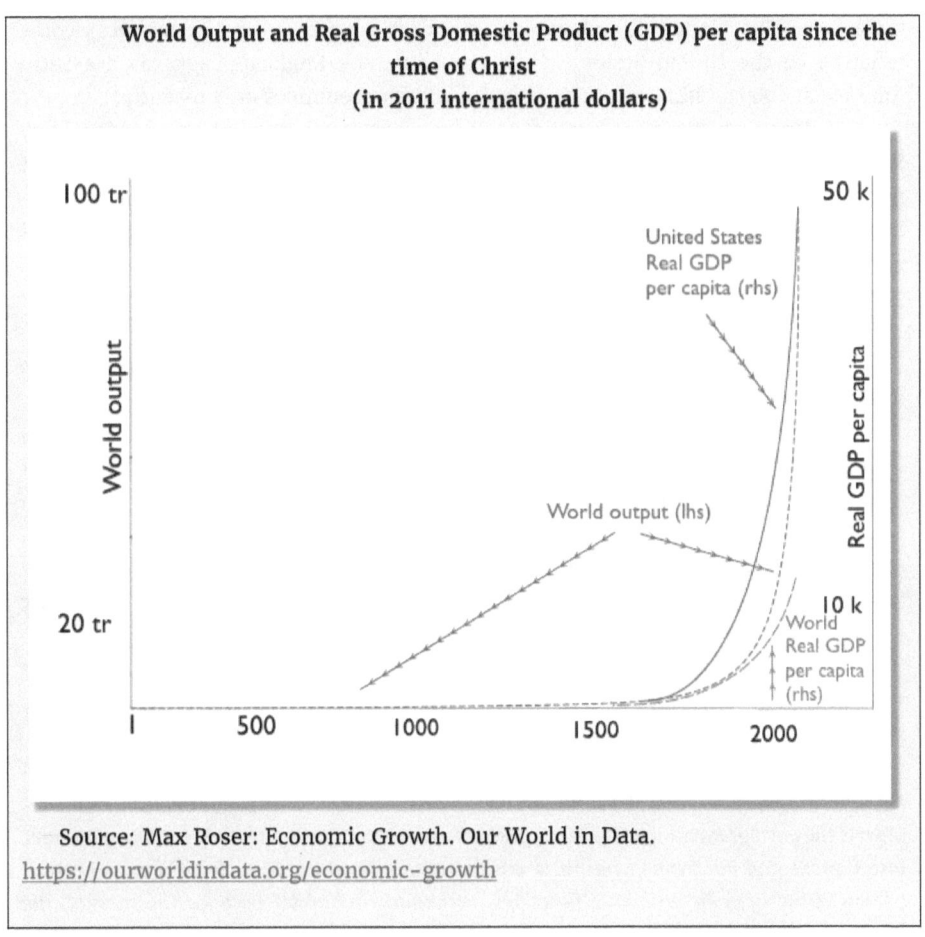

Source: Max Roser: Economic Growth. Our World in Data.
https://ourworldindata.org/economic-growth

Production as a process changed with the capitalist revolution. It is no coincidence that modern capitalism took off during the same period when slavery ended. Capital substituted human labor, and the machines replaced the slaves. In due course, capitalism abolished not only slavery but liberated also the women.

The graph shows total world output (left-hand side in trillions of international dollars) since the year 1. One can identify the take-off at the end of 18th century. Since then world output has reached one hundred trillion international dollars. The two other lines in the graph depict the real gross domestic product (GDP) per capita of the United States and of the world (in thousands of international dollars).

The transition from mass poverty to prosperity came with the industrial revolution. The United Kingdom was the first country to get a higher income followed by the United States, which soon overtook England. Laggards are Latin America and Asia. China and India have freed their economies only recently.

Japan was the first Asian country to adopt capitalist production followed by South Korea and many other countries, including China. Nevertheless, the recent newcomers have still a lot ahead in order to avoid remaining stuck at the middle-income level and catch-up to US-level with stands at roughly 50,000 international dollars per capita.

Backgrounder: Capital

The term 'capital' is a generic concept used in different meanings. Principle distinctions refer to 'physical', 'financial', 'human', and 'social' capital.

'Physical capital' exists in tools, machines, and the physical infrastructure. Physical capital is visible and tangible. It comprises heterogeneous pieces of goods that have 'multiple specificities' for the production process so that capital goods can be re-switched to a certain degree but are not full substitutes. One can, for example, use a hammer for different tasks. It has a 'multiple specificity' of limited range. The 'capital structure' exists as a complex of complementary goods whose unifying principle is not physical but exists in the mind of the entrepreneur.

Physical capital exists in the form of capital goods that are identifiable, yet which link the individual capital goods to each other as one can observe with the machines in a factory or the connections of a bridge with the roads.

Ludwig Lachmann explains: *"The generic concept of capital without which economists cannot do their work has no measurable counterpart among material objects; it reflects the entrepreneurial appraisal of such objects. Beer barrels and blast furnaces, harbour installations and hotel-room furniture are capital not by virtue of their physical properties but by virtue of their economic functions. Something is capital because the market, the consensus of entrepreneurial minds, regards it as capable of yielding an income. This does not mean that the phenomena of capital cannot be comprehended by clear and unambiguous concepts. The stock of capital used by society does not present a picture of chaos. Its arrangement is not arbitrary. There is some order in it.*" (Ludwig Lachmann: "Capital and Its Structure", 1956)

'Financial capital' is a concept that refers to the financial expression of assets. Financial capital exists as an accounting tool be it for a private or public enterprise or for a person or a family. The precondition of financial capital is money and accounting. Financial capital is a mental instrument of business management and serves for calculating one's assets in a homogeneous form.

'Human capital' is embodied in the individual person and exists in a person's skills, knowledge, and traits as they contribute to the production process. Different from physical capital, which suffers from depreciation over time, human capital tends to improve with its use.

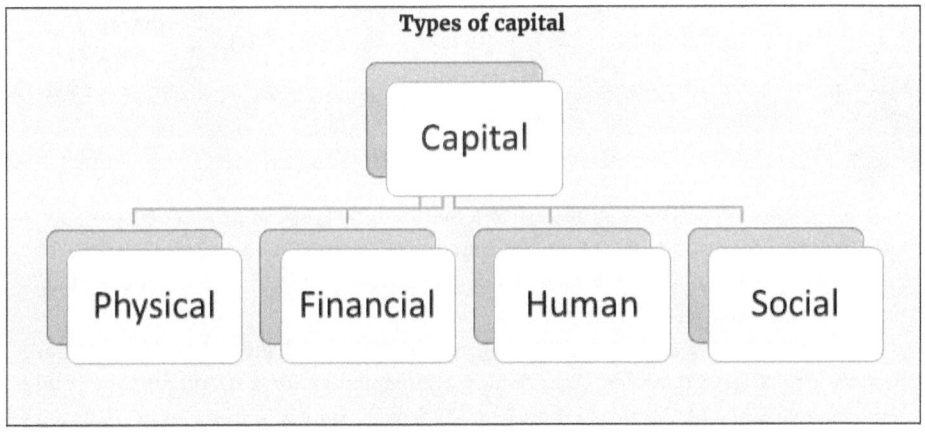

Social capital' - also called 'cultural capital' – represents the quality of the interrelation and interaction among the members of a society. 'Social capital' denotes the degrees and types of mutual trust (reciprocity) and societal cohesion as the precondition of market transactions. Around 1800, capitalist production took off. The capitalist production consists in the systematic use of capital and technology to widen and to improve the output.

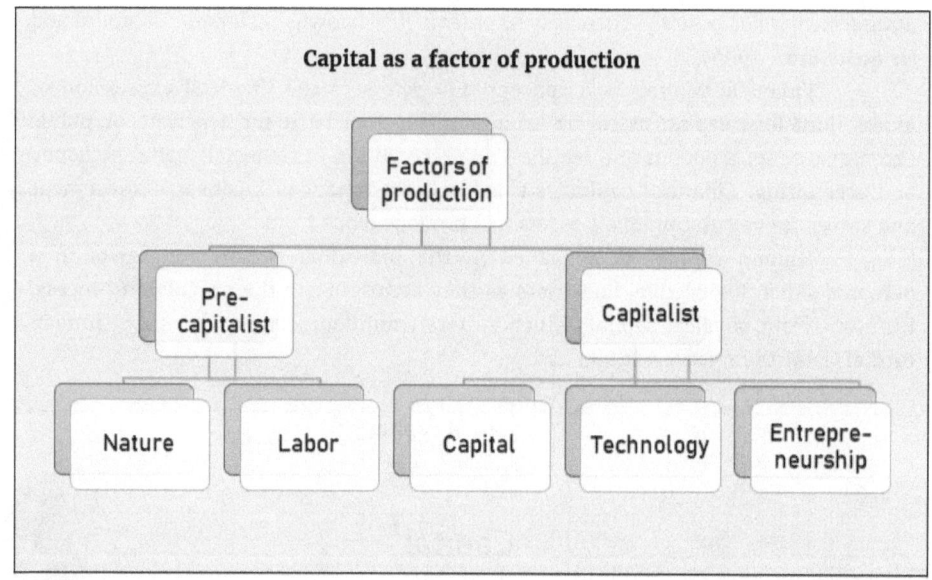

Capitalist production has led to a manifold increase of production per capita and has lifted the income to levels that exceeds any historical standards. The capitalist production marks a new era in the development of humankind and this period differs from all previous periods.

In as much as the modern economies have abolished slavery, they have become capitalist economies. Abandoning the capitalist form of production would imply the collapse of the production level. It would come along not only with mass poverty but also with mass starvation.

Development stages of capitalism

Not all countries take part in the history of capitalism.

In the period of 'take-off capitalism' led by England, most countries outside of Northern Europe and North America did not join and only when it showed how far they had fallen back did a reversal set it and these countries tried to catch-up. This holds also for parts of Southern and Eastern Europe. In Asia, Japan was the pioneer nation to adopt capitalism, while it took up to the 1990s of the 20th century for China to open its economy to markets. Take-off capitalism means mobilizing the factors of production, at first labor and capital.

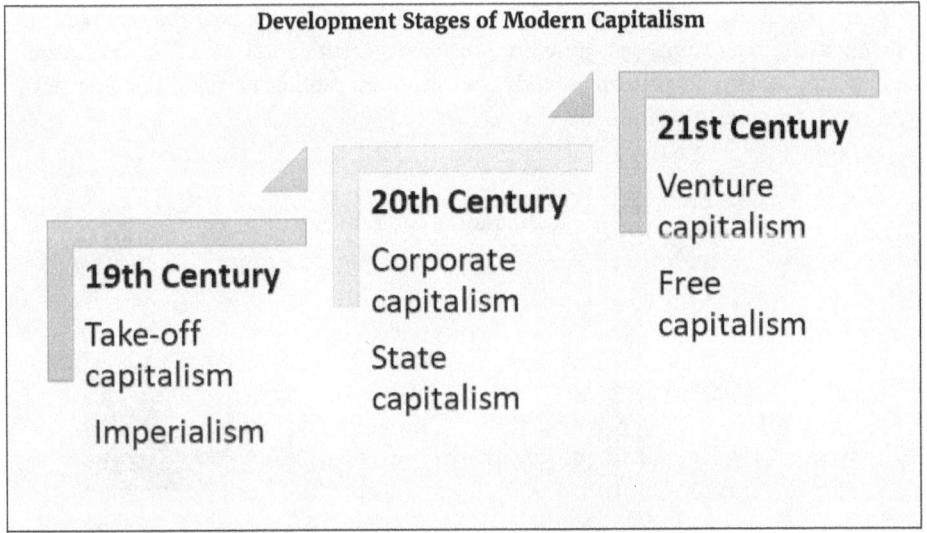

'Corporate capitalism' characterized the 20th century. It denotes the second stage after mobilizing the factors of production. Corporate capitalism concentrates on the efficiency of the use of the factors of production. The United States, Japan, and Germany are the most prominent members. These countries gained high rates of productivity in the organization of production and distribution by discipline and control. The Soviet Union, too, tried to achieve high productivity through discipline and control, yet failed because the Communists eliminated private property, profit, and market prices as the prime coordination mechanism and thus destroyed the tools of economic calculation.

'Venture capitalism' is the new stage of the capitalist development. Innovation dominates the emerging new forms of production. As the state recedes, entrepreneurship is on the rise. Connectivity substitutes organization and control and makes way for the spontaneous order that emerges on a local scale.

Not all countries will take part in the new stage. Not much different from at the time of 'take-off capitalism', certain societies reject creative destruction that comes with innovation and the new forms of doing business. The decline of the role of the nation-state will make way for local units to emerge with their proper kind of sovereignty and an individualistic political structure. The success of these new forms of production will invite imitation.

The alternative between socialism and capitalism as generic concepts does not exist. Socialism is a subcategory of capitalism. The point is whether more state or less state. Socialism is the strongest form of state capitalism while free capitalism is an economic system with least state and politics. It is also wrong to ask which system promises to offer more welfare and social security because the real point is productivity. The supposed difference between 'continental' and 'Anglo-Saxon' capitalism is also irrelevant as both are forms of capitalism typical of the 20th century's 'corporate capitalism'.

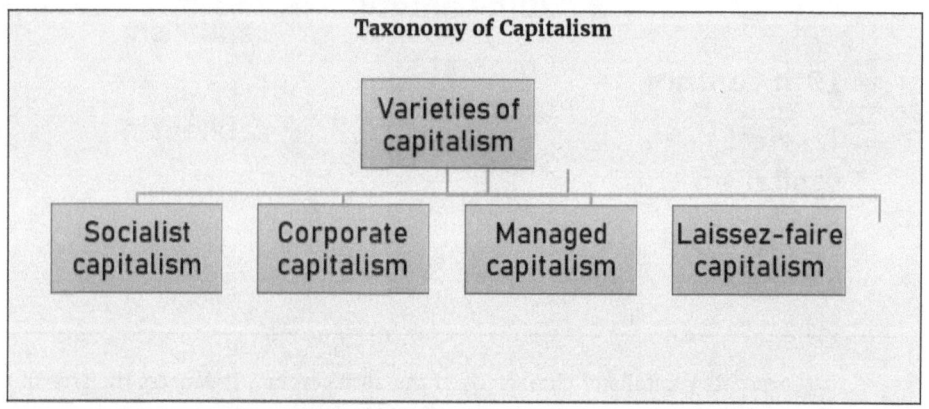

The historical movement goes from the left to the right but happens not without setbacks. Throughout history until the industrial revolution, the dominant system was socialist capitalism, and the socialism of the 20th century was tentative to restore the old system. Nostalgic feelings of a 'paradise lost' mark the socialists until our days. Outside of the socialist camp, the dominant system is 'corporate capitalism' in its many forms – including the welfare state. 'Managed capitalism' represents an advancement over interventionist capitalism as it tries to substitute general rules for discretionary policies as it is the case with monetary and fiscal policy rules. 'Ordo-liberalism' is such a tentative along with certain postulates that come under the label of 'neoliberalism'. Both these attempts must fail under the conditions of the modern system of democracy as a political party competition. 'Laissez-faire' capitalism is free capitalism. Its characteristic is the minimization and abolishment of the state and politics. This form of production requires 'demarchy' as a political system.

CAPITALISM AND THE STATE

The theoretical justification of the modern state, as elaborated by Thomas Hobbes (1588-1679) in his "Leviathan" (1651), postulates that people voluntarily succumb to the power of the state. In this model, the fear of anarchy drives people into submission. Yet Hobbes ignores that people want not only security but also seek prosperity and freedom. The more the state dominates our lives, the less is there a space for a free capitalism and thus for freedom and prosperity. Hobbes' state is not sustainable without the permanent use of force. Instead of establishing peace, the Hobbesian state brings violence, disunity, rebellion, and war. The Hobbesian state is a warfare state.

Between the extremes of a state, which forbids private ownership of the means of production and where the state holds the authority to manage the entire economy on the one hand, and free capitalism without state interventions on the other hand, there exist many mixed forms. The more socialist an economic system becomes the more people suffer not only material deprivation, but they lose also individual freedom. The more capitalist an economy, the more this society will enjoy freedom and prosperity.

Until the eighteenth century, the authorities almost everywhere in the world suppressed capitalism. Even today, political power is a constant threat to a free capitalism. The modern so-called 'mixed economy' exists as 'state capitalism' or as 'corporate capitalism'. In most countries, government tolerates capitalism only so far as it serves to enhance the power of the state. When modern capitalism manifested its productive capacity in the industrial revolution, the power of the state merged into a new system forming the dominant form of capitalism as state capitalism. Free capitalism will come to fruition not before the role of the state and of politics becomes minimal or vanishes altogether.

True capitalism is free capitalism. Free capitalism is a project of the future. Some countries are farther away from the capitalist ideal while other countries are closer to its pure form, but no country lives up to the ideal. Neither dictatorship nor democracy will automatically drive to free capitalism. Capitalism is still instrumental to the state. States use this form of production to promote the state's power. In the current system, the economy is subject to politics and the state. Most governments recognize that the more intense the competition in price-driven markets becomes, and the more there are entrepreneurial freedom and secure property rights, the wealthier this country will be. This is the path of the historical evolution. What has hitherto been the case will even be more valid in the future: the more a country approaches pure capitalism, the more prosperous it gets. Yet to achieve this goal, the state must give in and vanish.

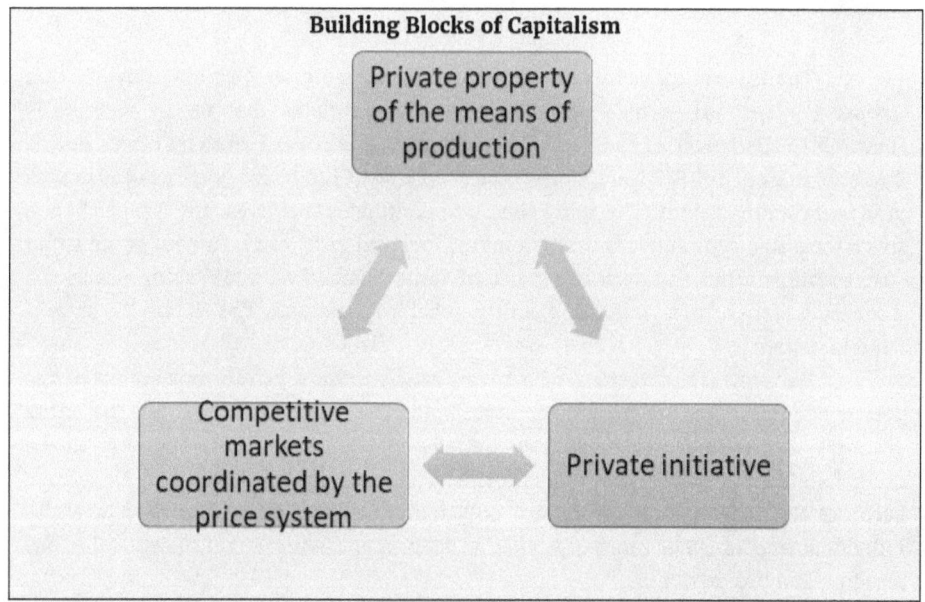

Modern capitalism rests on private ownership of the means of production. 'Capital' in this sense is the core of capitalism. Property rights are a necessary condition for capitalism to function, yet property alone is not sufficient for a proper working of a market economy. The working of a capitalist system requires that price-driven competitive markets accompany private ownership, and that there is a wide space for the private initiative.

The economy gets more productive, the more secure the private property is, the more price-driven the competitive markets are, and the more there is freedom for the private initiative.

***

Liberal capitalism opposes communism and socialism and is not compatible with Nazism either. A motto, such as that of the National Socialist Workers' Party (NSDAP), 'public interest before self-interest' or the motto of the Hitler Youth (HJ): 'You are nothing, your nation is everything' runs against the spirit of a free economy. A free economy and the personal self-determination result when the individual can pursue his own interests. This not the case with totalitarianism. The credo as exposed by the Italian fascist leader Benito Mussolini (1883-1945): 'All within the state, nothing outside the state, nothing against the state' is the opposite of the libertarian position. The most powerful institutions in the socialist countries - whether they are national-socialist or international-socialist - are the respective unitary party and the military. Other social institutions, up to the family, are subject to the dictates of the system. The Third Reich was just as much a military state as the Soviet Union.

The driving force behind the capitalist system is the private initiative. The historical experience demonstrates that where there are free markets that provide space for the individual initiative, where the property rights are safe, and the tax burden is low, prosperity thrives. When, however, the state restricts the individual rights, and when the state' bureaucracy suppress the private initiative, there is economic, social and cultural decline.

Economic stagnation results when business is losing its freedom to act because of excessive regulations and of high taxes. New companies will not arise under these restrictions. Then the production becomes more expensive, the entrepreneurial spirit weakens, and investment and innovation wane. The economy stagnates, and the society impoverishes.

Antony P. Mueller

WHAT ARE CAPITALISTS GOOD FOR?

In the market economy, a vote takes place with every purchase. By deciding to buy this specific product and not another one, the consumers elect those companies that manufacture this good to go on with their production. By this vote, the consumers chose these companies and entrepreneurs to lead the production process. The ballot in capitalism consists in money, the vote is the purchase. The capitalists are the legal owners of the production resources such as gas stations, restaurants, and shopping malls, yet they only earn a yield on their capital stock by making their property available to the use by the customers. By purchasing the product, the customers determine the value of the capital, which serves to produce this good. Like consumer goods, production goods, too, have no intrinsic value. The price of capital goods reflects their capacity to produce goods, which customers want and will pay for.

The capitalists must maintain and improve the capital stock in order to earn a profit. Stores require maintenance; airplanes need checks and services; machines need repairs. Capitalists must bear the costs of preserving and adapting the capital structure. For this maintenance of keeping the capital structure intact, capitalists make advance payments. They assume the risk as to the uncertainties surrounding the future yield. While the workers receive their salaries right away, the capitalist get their compensation not before the good reaches the final consumer and gets paid. While the workers receive their remuneration during the production process before the goods reach the consumers, the capitalists bear both the initial costs and the risks of whether the capital goods will bring income in the end. The yield comes only when the end user pays for the goods. Whether an investment will have an economic value depends on the extent to which it contributes to producing goods that consumers want and will buy.

HOW CAPITALISM CREATES WEALTH & PROMOTES PROSPERITY

The customer expects that shops will provide a rich offer from which to choose. Hardly anyone wonders who keeps the store in operation and who makes sure that a variety of goods is available. Few customers spend a thought how much capital the capitalists put at the service for the customers before a buyer pays. If the government and its bureaucracy substitute capitalism or regulate, harass and confiscate the capitalists, it does not take long, and the capital structure will disintegrate. All it takes is to diminish the profit expectations of the capitalists and the capital structure crumbles.

Large wealth exists in company stocks or in other forms of participation in companies. Wealth comes from investments, and investments come from savings. More savings mean less consumption. The wealth of the owners of a supermarket chain are their stores. The stockholders are the owners. Yet who are the actual beneficiaries of the stores? Those people who shop in these stores and enjoy the products offered.

A considerable number of the super-rich people pursue a modest lifestyle. Part of the financial success of these persons comes because of being thrifty and not to waste but to save and invest. Even a great fortune cannot last long when it gets into the hands of a hedonistic spendthrift. Wealth abhors high time-preference and stays with those who know how to economize.

The market itself takes care that wealth accumulation will not go on forever and accumulate in one or only a few hands. The profitability of a company is under constant threat from innovation. From the wealth of the railway barons at the end of the nineteenth century there is little left today. The Ford, Rockefeller, and Vanderbilt families, and the inheritors of the wealth of the other tycoons of the past have vanished from the top list of the wealthy. While Wal Mart seemed well established only a short time ago, it now faces a challenge from online shopping.

There will always be a group of super rich people, yet under capitalism, the composition among those who make up the high-wealth people, changes. In capitalism, innovation does away with old wealth. As such, capitalism differs from the economic systems of the past. Historically, to own land was the foundation of wealth. Before the industrial revolution, the main source of wealth was ownership in land, which formed the basis for inheritance. The titles on the property came along with the title of nobility and other social rank distinctions. In pre-capitalist times, the rich were the same families for long periods, and almost all those who were born poor were to remain poor.

If one compares the list of the super-rich, which the magazine Forbes publishes annually, few names – if any - show up over a longer period. The people of wealth change with the lines of business. Until the 1980s, there were no super-rich people from the software, electronics and computer sectors on the list, as they are now the broadest group because these production areas were only just at the beginning of their triumph. Now, names from this area dominate the list as in earlier times the owners of railway or oil companies made up the list a hundred years ago.

***

FORBES List of Top 10 Billionaires

First FORBES List of Top 10 Billionaires (1987)
Taikichiro Mori/property development
Yoshiaki Tsutsumi/transport, hotels
Yohachiro Iwasaki/logging, property
Shigeru Kobayashi/real estate
Haruhiko Yoshimoto/real estate
Brenninkmeyer family/retailing
Hans and Gad Rausing/liquid packaging
Albert, Paul, Ralph Reichmann/real estate
Kenneth Roy Thomson/media, petroleum
Eitaro Itoyama/property

2017 FORBES List of Top 10 billionaires
Bill Gates/software
Warren Buffett/investment
Jeff Bezos/online retailing
Amancio Ortega/retailing
Mark Zuckerberg/social media
Carlos Slim/cell phone
Larry Ellison/computer
David Koch/industrial conglomerate
Michael Bloomberg/financial information

Forbes' first list of 1987 was dominated by Japanese real estate tycoons, a group that has vanished from the 2017 list.

Source: https://www.forbes.com/billionaires/#5b3b1c97251c

***

Modern capitalism is an entrepreneurial capitalism. Its motor is innovation. Innovation brings with it ongoing structural change so that exceptional wealth eminence does not last long. Companies emerge and disappear, and the wealth of individuals and families grows and goes with them.

Today's wealth is ownership of stocks. How stocks perform, determine the wealth of the owners. Equity markets evaluate companies and thus determine the individual wealth of the owners of these companies. Becoming part of the club of the capitalists is open to everyone. One can buy individual stocks or investment funds. Start-ups go public and may offer opportunities for the investors willing to take higher risks. Modern capitalism is popular capitalism. It is a capitalism by the people and for the people. Modern capitalism realizes the socialist dream that the workers themselves become proprietors. This happens under capitalism through the stock market.

Antony P. Mueller

THE STOCK MARKET WITHOUT PUZZLES

The stock exchange is a central institution of modern capitalism. Stock markets emerge with modern monetary capitalism. They had their first flourishing in Amsterdam and later in London. Today, New York is the center of the global stock trading. A stock market is a trading place. As to which types of assets and goods are the object of the trade, there exist commodity, foreign exchange, bond market markets, and the stock exchange. Exchanges are markets where supply meets demand and where the price formation takes place. It is wrong to take the price of a security as its value. A specific stock market price indicates that at a certain point in time and space, purchases and sales took place at this definite price. The so-called 'stock market value' of a company does not represent the 'value' of this company. As a price, the stock market valuation of an asset fluctuates with the trades at the stock exchange.

Of the total existing stocks, bonds, and commodities, only a small part trades in a session. It is therefore misleading to take the stock market quotation at face value to determine the 'value' of the entire company, as it is done, for example, when one calculates the so-called 'capitalization' of companies. This inappropriate approach is already obsolete at when the results get published. Stock market quotations are changing even if nothing spectacular happens to the company that the share represents because some people sell and buy.

The intense observation of the price quotations is useful when one wants to buy or to sell and is on the look-out for a good timing. The momentary quotations are important for the market professionals, yet for the investor, the short-term quotations are of little significance. What counts is being in the market and to earn the dividend in the long run. The dividends of stocks and the interest payments of bonds are the sources of the income for the capitalist - different from the speculator who wants to profit from the price changes and the market professionals who live from the trades.

There is a debate in finance about the determinants of the stock market prices. The dispute rages between representatives of the efficient market hypothesis (EMH) and the behavioral theorists.

The adherents of the efficient market hypothesis claim that the stock price itself is the best expression of the present value as it reflects the state of the obtainable information. Only new information changes the price. Therefore, stock market prices move in a random way as the information comes in. As an argument against the efficiency hypothesis, one can hold that the market is not perfect since people are not perfect, and markets are no more and no less 'information-efficient' than human beings can be information efficient. It is not 'the information' that makes the price, but the human decision to buy or to sell according to the individual evaluation of the information.

At the other extreme, the behavioral theory of asset markets is wrong because it tries to explain human action in the light of a psychology of irrationality. Yet what may seem irrational to the observer does not have to be irrational for the actor himself. Extreme fluctuations of the prices are not irrational, for example, when the market is narrow and when the participants change their views about how to assess the future profitability of a company. The efficient market hypothesis underestimates the costs of getting information.

The stock exchange has an anchor with the company profits. In order to distribute dividends, the company must generate profits. The main determinant of the price of a company's stock is its profit position relative to that of alternative investments and the respective expectations. Therefore, the current price of a share depends not only on the individual company but also on the profit situation and the profits of other companies and on the potential income and risks of alternative investments. The individual stock price is connected to the local stock and to the national markets and to all potential investments around the world and their respective currencies.

The price of an individual share, as well as the status of the securities market represented in its index, results from the valuations of all potential investments in the financial markets and their embeddedness in the national and global environment. Therefore, it is impossible to predict the movements of individual shares or the stock market index consistently. Yet such forecasts are also unnecessary because the main advantage of investing in stocks is to participate in the growth of the economy and to maintain at the same time high liquidity. Unlike real estate, for example, one can convert stocks into cash fast and also in small or in large quantities on the stock exchange. In this respect, the stock market investment is unique and provides advantages that no other kind of investment can offer.

The daily stock trading represents the so-called 'secondary market' in contrast to the market for new emissions in the form of initial public offerings (IPO) or the issue of new stocks by an established company to increase its capital base. Secondary market means that only a part of the investment holdings is available for trade. Depending on which side - whether demand or supply - there is more urgency, the prices will rise or fall. If the supply is tight, and the demand increases, the prices will rise. When demand falls and supply increases, prices drop. Sometimes the market is 'thin' because only light trading is going on. Under such a condition, the urgent need of liquidity by some market participants can provoke strong price cuts. This day-to-day trading is unpredictable and does not violate the principle of the theory - neither that of the efficient market hypothesis nor that of the behavioral financial economics. It is impossible to predict an individual event with certainty.

Long periods of a bull market (rising prices) or a bear market (falling prices) come about depending on whether more money flows into the stock market or more money leaves the market. This inflow and outflow reflect the tides of the amount of money that circulates in the economy and of the investment alternatives and their returns and their risks.

Booms of the stock market with the tendency of a bubble occur when the central bank floods the economy with money at a time when the real economy offers few attractive alternative investments. A bear market happens when liquidity shrinks or when many new investment opportunities arise in the real economy. Then there is a general lack of money or money remains outside of the stock exchange to finance business transactions. If securities owners want to sell with urgency in such a situation, they can do so only at low prices. Such a constellation offers opportunities for the buyer of stocks. The time to make a fortune is in the bear market.

The price movement of stocks is paradoxical because it often runs contrary to the tendency in the real economy. In the long run, however, stock prices depend on the growth of the real economy, since the purpose of holding securities is to earn dividends and the dividend payments depend on corporate profits.

As an owner of shares, the investor is at the origin of the wealth creation of the capitalist economy. Other forms of income depend on the wealth that the corporate world creates. Employment and income arise from and through the profits of companies. For the banks to pay interest on savings, they must generate income by granting loans to companies and consumers. For the state to pay interest on its bonds, the government must earn tax receipts that depend on profits, wages, and sales. In order to be able to employ workers, companies must make profitable deals. Before the government can spend, they need to tax. Government expenditure depends on the profits and the incomes in the private sector.

Since the 1980s, there has been a large increase in the financial sector of the economy. This growth of finance is evident in the USA. The growth of the financial sector coincides with the increase of the money supply and the rise of government debt. What some call 'casino capitalism' has its basis in the growth of the public debt and in monetary inflation. When the growth of government debt and of the money supply reach their limits, the share of the financial sector will decline, and the price levels of the securities will normalize.

Investment Strategies

The table below highlights the performance of various assets under different macroeconomic constellations. Overall, stocks perform well not only in an environment of low stable but also in periods of expansionary deflation and expansionary inflation. Bonds do well in an expansionary disinflation and a deflationary contraction while gold protects against global stagflation. The best time for commodities are in periods of expansionary inflation while real estate performs well when there is a low and stable inflation and in times of expansionary inflation.

Macroeconomic Constellations and Investment Strategy

	Stocks	Bonds	Real Estate	Gold	Commodities
Low Stable Inflation	+	0	+	0	0
Expansionary Disinflation	+	+	0	0	0
Deflationary Contraction	-	+	0	0	-
Global Stagflation	-	-	-	+	-
Local Stagflation	-	-	-	-	-
Expansionary Inflation	+	-	+	0	+

Although real estate prices do not always decline and rise parallel to the stock market, they are not separate from the economic performance of the national economy. Unlike stocks and real estate, however, bonds and monetary savings suffer from inflation. Although the investment in gold protects against inflation, gold brings no current returns. One must sell gold to earn a yield on this investment.

As a general rule, one can say that the enemies of the stock market are the same as those of a prosperous economy. Besides the outright enemies such as socialization and nationalization, the hidden enemies comprise a higher price inflation, rising interest rates, and a growing public debt.

The US stock market exhibits a long bull market period from 1870 to the First World War, a strong recovery towards the end of the 1920s and the long bear market of the Great Depression. It took over two decades for the stocks to return to the level before the Great Depression began. After the long postwar period, a bear market happened again during the stagflation in the 1970s. Since 1982, there has been a mega bull market, which experienced a slight interruption in the years from 2000 to 2008 only to re-surge again since then.

In the case of bear market periods, one must consider that when stock prices are low, equities have a low price-earnings ratio (P/E). Price-earnings ratios of less than ten, for example, say that those shares will recover their price in ten years through profits and the dividends they distribute. Stock market crashes do not imply that the investors go empty.

There is no such thing as a safe investment. Those investors who fear stock market crashes and panics and buy real estate or bonds instead cannot avoid losses when the political and social environment falls into chaos. Ultimately, the return on economic investments depends on how profitable the companies are. When these fail, everything else also falls to pieces

***

Through the ownership of shares, the investor takes part in business and is at the place where the national wealth comes from. The yield of other investments - be it bonds, real estate or art - depends on the overall economic performance, i.e. the profit situation of the companies. This also applies to the public systems of old-age pensions. What counts is the extent to which the economy produces the goods and services that the pensioner needs in retirement.

COMMERCE

To increase prosperity, one needs, first, accumulation of capital, more and better tools; second, human capital: the skills of the people to produce goods and services; third, innovation: to apply ideas on how to make the things people want and need; and four, commerce: the exchange of goods to enable the specialization of capital and labor. When these factors occur together, economic progress happens. The effectiveness of each of these factors depends on commerce, on freedom that exists in the realm of the exchange of goods and services in the markets. As commerce requires a free market economy, prosperity requires a free market system.

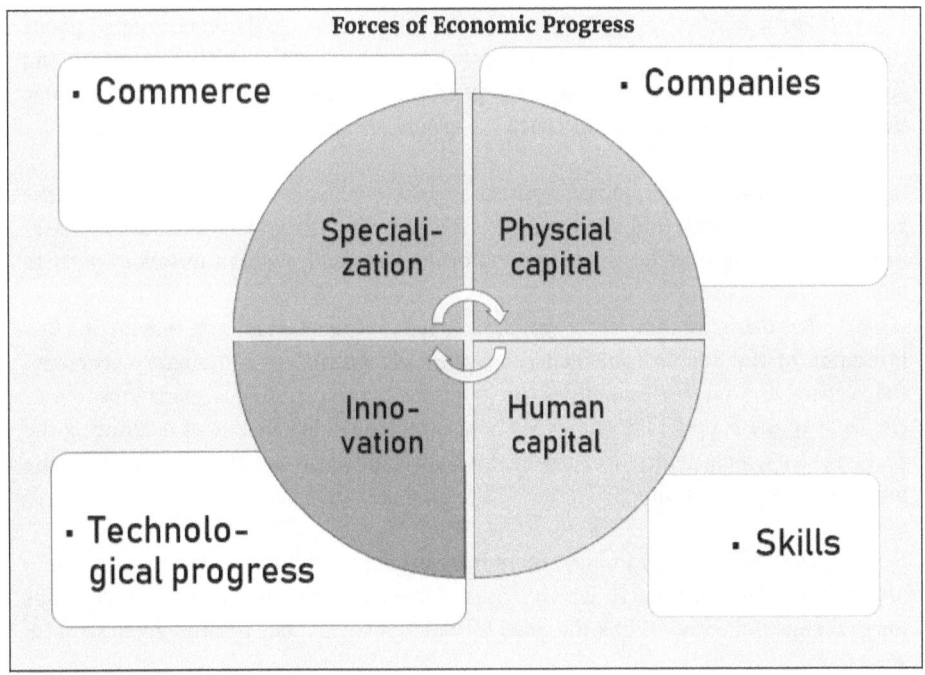

More prosperity comes from higher productivity. Specialization of labor and capital requires commerce. Firms are places of specialization of labor and capital. Companies provide capital while the workers and employees contribute their knowledge in the form of human capital. Technological progress means to realize new business ideas. These ideas will become profitable through entrepreneurial innovations.

All four factors are interrelated.

The more intensive the trade, the more accumulation of capital is possible.

The more capital is available, the more effective is the knowledge.

The larger the stock of physical and human capital, the more innovation comes.

With technical progress, productivity grows, and prosperity increases.

***

The more intensive the commerce, the more specialization is possible. The potential of specialization grows with the size of the market. What begins at the level of a simple exchange within the family and the local market continues at the regional and national levels, to embrace the whole globe.

For a market to expand beyond the neighborhood, the exchange of goods requires money. Money is productive because it facilitates the exchange of goods and services. Without money, the exchange possibilities would be limited and thus also the specialization and the productivity.

Without money, barter requires a 'double coincidence of wants', since the vendor must not only find someone who wants to buy his goods, but the purchaser must at the same time be someone who offers the good, which the seller wants to buy.

By using money as a general means of exchange and payment, this limitation of the double coincidence of wants disappears. In a monetary economy, the respective producer exchanges his goods for money and thus gains freedom of choice as to the suppliers of the goods he wants. Money is a means of facilitating the exchange of goods, which in turn enables specialization and thereby provides the foundation of productivity.

In the absence of money, there is no exchange of goods between A, B, and C. Although A offers the good X, which B asks, B does not have the good Y, which A asks for exchange. Likewise, C has the good Y, which A wants, but not the good X that B wants.

Exchange by barter and by money

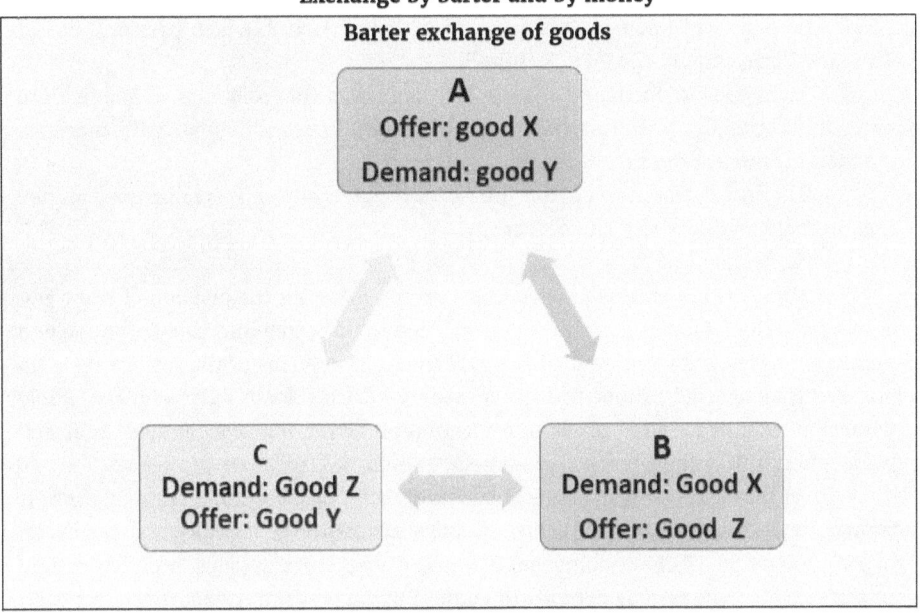

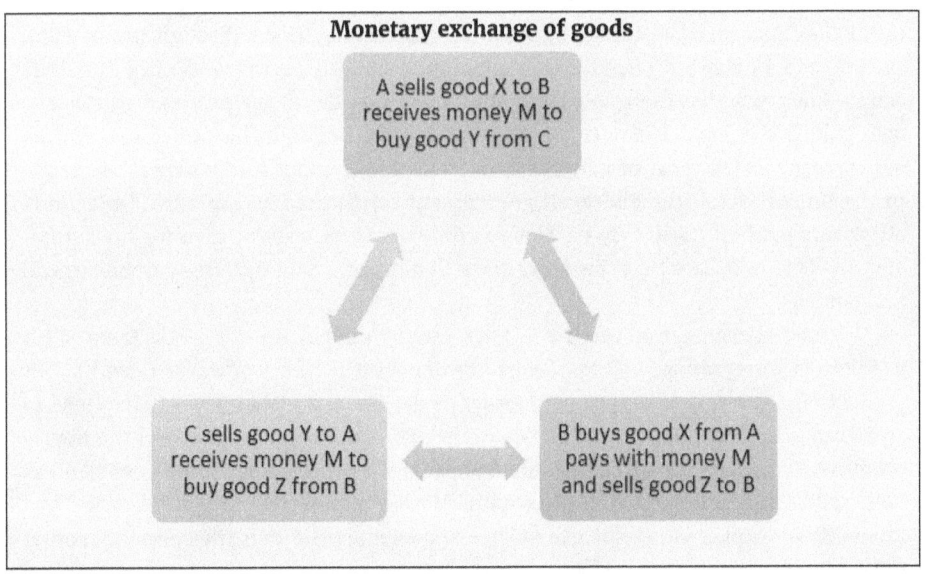

After introducing money as a general means of exchange, the problem of the so-called 'double coincidence of wants' finds its solution. Person *A* sells the good X to B who pays with money. Person *A* demands the good Y, which person C has to offer, and C can acquire the good Z from B.

Money is productive. It allows and facilitates the exchange of goods. Pure barter limits the size of the market. Exchange through money comes with markets, and market transactions create the monetary prices.

The larger the market, the greater the potential for specialization. Money thus promotes productivity and prosperity.

***

Money is not sterile because it is a precondition for the division of labor and of specialization. Money is an instrument of rational economic calculation. When production exceeds its simple forms, the calculation in terms of natural goods is no longer sufficient. One cannot add up cheese, wine, and horse-carts and the whole plethora of other economic goods in a meaningful sense, but one can add, subtract, divide and multiply their respective monetary sums.

While money is instrumental to the division of labor and for calculation, it cannot serve as a 'storage of value' because all future consumption depends on future production. The economy as a whole cannot save today's production and conserve it for the years or decades to come. Buildings disintegrate, machines rust, food spoils. Most services - be it a medical treatment or a haircut - require that production takes place simultaneously with consumption. The future level of consumption depends on the future circumstances of the production. Money cannot fulfill the function of a storage of value because money flows through the banking system and borrowers spend the money that the lender saves. Money hoarders cannot know whether their notes will still be legal tender in the future or whether to own gold is still legal. Many countries have experienced monetary reforms with the old currency losing most of its purchasing power and sometimes losing all its value. In the United States, the Roosevelt government confiscated by Executive Order 6102 all private gold on April 5, 1933. There is only one sure way to 'save for the future' and this is to take care that the dark time will not come, and that free capitalism will prosper.

An economy can reach a higher output mobilizing the labor force - for example by integrating women. While the increase in the workforce does not lift productivity in terms of output per worker or per hour, it would nevertheless lead to an increase in the national income per capita. The output per worker and the hourly productivity depend on specialization. Specialization of the labor force goes hand in hand with the specialization of the capital. With a high degree of specialization and intensive division of labor, the use of special machines and thus the specialization of the capital is also intensive.

Companies are places of specialization. The more specialized a company is, the more it is worthwhile for this company to use special tools and to employ technical and administrative specialists. The key to prosperity is productivity. All differences in race, gender, and geographic location disappear regarding time. For everyone, the number of hours per day is the same. No human being can permanently work over eight or ten hours each day. More wealth by more work has a natural limit. Unlimited wealth creation comes through rising productivity.

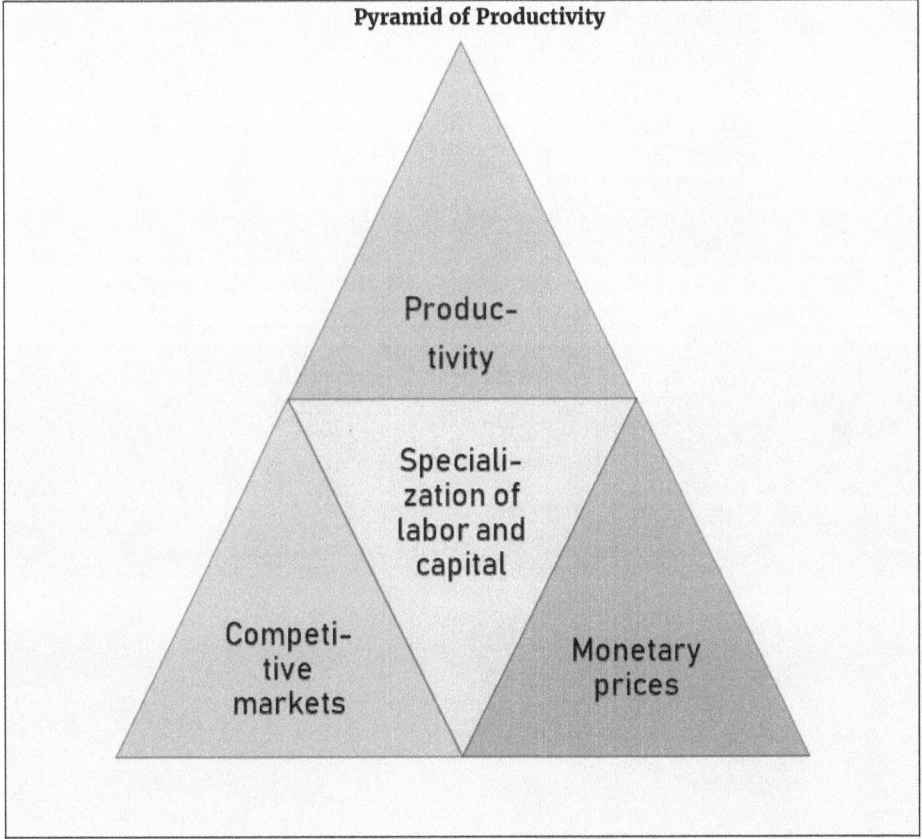

Productivity grows with specialization, and specialization of both capital and labor takes place in companies.

Productivity increases prosperity. Money is productive in the sense that it allows specialization and price calculation.

Interventions, which disrupt the functioning of the markets and affect the monetary system, are harmful because they affect the specialization and thus reduce productivity and lead to loss of prosperity.

MONETARY ECONOMY

Modern capitalism is an entrepreneurial capitalism. The cradle of modern capitalism were the factories and workshops run by entrepreneurs as the place to combine capital, labor, and knowledge. Firms are the source of productivity and prosperity. The prevalence of modern capitalism, as it has developed since the industrial revolution, is the spread of private firms around the world. The obvious characteristic of our time compared to the situation of two hundred years ago is the number, size, and importance of business companies.

If one wants to give the term 'capitalism' a specific meaning, then it is about a wide network of profit-seeking firms. In modern capitalism, there are not only large companies active but even more so also medium, small, and micro-enterprises. The Marxists were wrong with their prediction that capitalism would bring with it a growing class of proletarians and a shrinking class of capitalists. A broad middle class is the hallmark of modern capitalism. If the middle class is small or shrinking, this is a sign that something is wrong with the economic system of this country.

The market competition takes place within a network of cooperation. A characteristic feature of the modern entrepreneurial economy is that the markets coordinate both competition and cooperation. The modern economy is a network of specialized units. The more complex and denser the network, the higher is the degree of possible specialization and the higher is the level of productivity.

The individual companies compete to produce the best products as cost-effectively as possible so that a company can make a profit. A firm attains this goal by way of cooperation with other companies as it embeds itself in the web of specialization and the exchange of goods. Capitalism is as much cooperation as it is competition. Cooperation happens within the company through the collaboration of the workforce and extends to the cooperation among different companies. An economy exists as a network of firms. The more a company specializes, the more it depends on suppliers. Cooperation does not exclude the competition but forms part of it. This cooperation, of course, can make it difficult for anti-monopolistic competition policy to single out market and price collusion. The market supervisors will raise false accusations of cartelization and collusion when they are not aware of that cooperation is an inherent feature of competition. The best policy against cartelization is an open market access and technological change and not an arbitrary policy intervention in the name of 'anti-cartelization' and 'competition' policy.

Companies can achieve extraordinary profits through innovation. This way, there is a continuous incentive to improve the offer of new and better goods and services. If these conditions prevail, monopolies are not only harmless but they also play an important role in the economic progress as the pioneers of innovation. The more open the market access, the less 'competition policy' is necessary.

The modern economy is a monetary economy. Modern capitalism is an 'entrepreneurial capitalism' that takes place in a monetary economy. Entrepreneurship is fundamental not only because of the role of companies as an economic unit of economic activity but also as the driving force behind economic growth, which is to accumulate capital and to realize innovation.

Entrepreneurship has redesigned the world. Prosperity has become universal. The beneficiaries of modern capitalism have been the ordinary people. In advanced industrial societies, the standard of living of a family with an average income surpasses the level of the living standard of the royal families of the past. The ordinary worker enjoys better living conditions than the nobility of the past. Electricity, refrigerator, washing machine, television, telephone, and an automobile have become common utensils in almost any household in the industrialized countries.

Progress, however, affects not only material things but also leisure. In the past, leisure time was not only rare but also not much exciting because there were few things to enjoy in the spare time other than to rest or get drunk. The time of youth was short, the adulthood full of hard work, and the old age burdened with frailty and boredom. Today, a considerable part of the economic output of an advanced economy consists in producing leisure goods. Capitalism creates not only material prosperity. By reducing the working hours, vast new possibilities have emerged for the productive enjoyment of the leisure time.

EQUALITY IS NOT JUSTICE

Modern happiness research shows that the greatest effect on the increase of well-being due to rising income happens when moving up from the low to the middle-income strata. When incomes rise above the levels of the upper middle class, further income increases are no longer associated with significant gains of personal happiness. While satisfaction continues to rise, the marginal increases in happiness diminish the higher one climbs up on the wealth ladder.

The material progress from no bed to one bed is much more valuable than to own a house with several bedrooms to choose from as a place to sleep. To escape hunger has a much greater individual benefit than being able to afford double or triple portions. The marginal benefit of the second TV or the third car to the well-being of the family is much lower than the benefit that came with the first TV set and the first automobile. The rate of the increase in happiness, therefore, decreases per unit of money as the material wealth grows. The millionaire or billionaire is not a million-fold or a billion-fold happier than the average wage earner.

According to the results of Jason Schnittker's research on the economics of happiness of the University of Pennsylvania, the marginal effect of income decreases for all categories of 'well-being'.

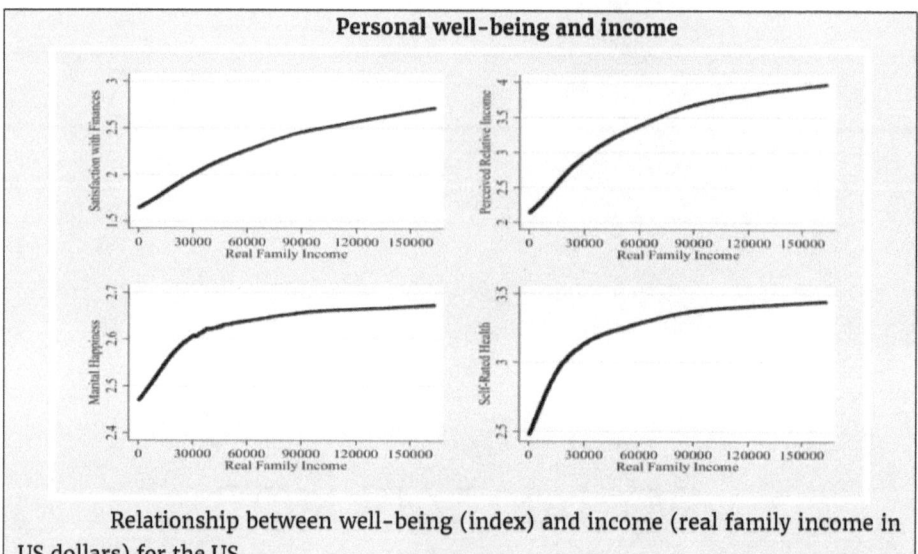

Relationship between well-being (index) and income (real family income in US dollars) for the US

Source: Jason Schnittker, Diagnosing our national disease: Trends in income and happiness, 1973 to 2004, American Sociological Association.

This result is most visible in the categories 'marital happiness' (graphic below left) and 'self-clarified state of health' (right below).

The diminishing marginal rate for 'satisfaction with the financial situation' (top left) and the assessment of the relative income (upper right) is less pronounced.

Further research shows that America's super-rich people are only marginally, and by no means all, more satisfied than the average well-to-do American.

That more money does not contribute to a sharp increase in happiness from an income, which corresponds to the upper middle class, but serves for other motives such as self-expression or self-realization, for example, means that one should not attach too much importance to inequality. In a capitalist economic system, the poor are better-off, and that the country has a strong middle class.

***

The discussion about equality and inequality of wealth and income has turned into an ideological battlefield. Most of the debate is beside the point. The heart of the matter is not how much more the super-rich earn and possess compared to the ordinary wage earner, but the core of the problem is to reduce poverty. It was the improvement of the fate of the poor where modern capitalism achieved its greatest triumphs. One cannot eradicate mass poverty without capitalism.

The decline in extreme poverty has come about because more countries have turned to the capitalist economic order as has been the case in China and Eastern Europe since the 1990s. During this development, income worldwide has risen, and its distribution has widened.

Before the triumph of monetary profit-oriented entrepreneurial capitalism, most of the people of a country were poor, while it is a minority in industrialized countries today. Even these poor people have a higher level of prosperity than the rich social classes of the past.

Elimination of Poverty

While about 95% of the world's population of the one billion people who lived before the Industrial Revolution suffered from extreme poverty, this figure fell below 10% by 2015. During this same period, world population has risen to over seven billion.

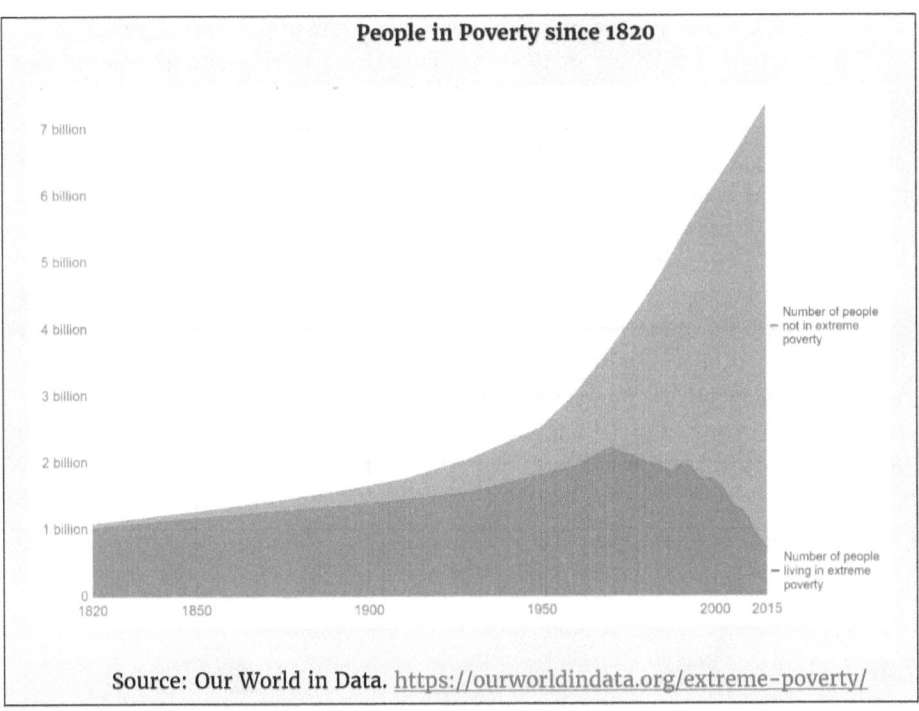

In the period since 1980, the number of people living in poverty (according to the line established by the World Bank) has fallen from close to 90 percent to under 10 percent.

***

The more capitalism has spread across the globe, however imperfect it still is, the more a middle-class has emerged, and the lower the number of people in extreme poverty has become. In China, poverty has been falling when the country changed course and moved to a capitalist system. A similar development takes place in India. Although in India, there never has been an outright communism, India practiced development socialism and is just beginning to reduce the influence, which the government exerts over the economy. The more India will abandon its old way, the faster misery will disappear as well as in the other countries that change their prevailing economic system to more capitalism.

China and India at a crossroads

Since the economic reforms and the move to a market economy, China gross domestic product per capita at purchasing power parity has grown from under 2,000 dollars to over 14,000 dollars per year.

India, whose gross domestic product per capita at purchasing power parity was similar to that of China in 1990, has increased its per capita income to over 6,000 dollars, less than half of that of China.

Both countries, China and India, face the challenge of going on with pro-market reforms against political obstacles and to avoid of getting stuck in the middle-income trap. Both China and India must go ahead with political reforms and curb the role of the state, of the bureaucracy, and of party politics. Yet it seems that China is taking the opposite direction.

The attempt of the ruling Communist Party of China to impose a comprehensive system of surveillance and control will abort the economic take-off and lead to economic stagnation with the income per capita staying low. In this respect, China would not be the first developing county that experienced a dramatic take-off yet remains stuck in the middle-income trap. The outcome of the race between India and China is still open.

***

ORIGINS OF WESTERN CAPITALISM

    The inception of modern capitalism took place towards the end of the 18th century. Nevertheless, the foundations for the industrial revolution existed before. The ground-breaking invention, which laid the cornerstone for the modern world, was, besides establishing the principles of double bookkeeping by the Franciscan monk Luca Bartolomeo de Pacioli in 1494, the invention of the printing press with movable letters by Johannes Gutenberg around 1450.
    The double-entry bookkeeping system promoted the rational management of a business enterprise, and from then on, with the printing press in place, it was possible to make ideas accessible to interested parties at a fraction of the former costs. Until the spread of the modern printing press, reading and writing were a privilege of the authorities and reserved to the upper clergy and to high officials who could exercise a comprehensive control over the people. Few common people learned to read. As long as the costs of books and of other reading material were beyond the reach of most people, this skill was of little use. With the spread of the printing press, the affordable access to reading material made it worthwhile for the public to learn to read.
    In 1517, the proclamation of Martin Luther's theses in Wittenberg started a strong incentive for learning to read. The Reformation proclaimed the personal study of the Bible as an obligation for the believers. Because there was no central authority, the new creed took hold in the individual geographical units, primarily at first in the independent city-states in the Northern parts of Europe. Books, pamphlets, and articles about God and the world spread across Europe, whereas the

Chinese emperor and the Sultanate of the Islamic world would suppress what seemed to endanger their autocratic rule. Europe differed from other regions of the world through the unity of a common language for the educated in form of the Latin of the Church, yet politically Europe comprised many individual political units of a diverse composition in which free, independent cities played an important role as autonomous political institutions. The attempts to control written material and to forbid the modern printing press failed in Europe - unlike as it was the case in many other regions of the world, where censorship prevailed. The 'Great Divergence' began when Europe took off, while these regions consequently fell back relative to Europe in terms of economic prosperity, scientific progress, and individual liberty.

***

Economic, technical and scientific progress lives on ideas. Yet ideas do not spread by themselves. Equally important as the idea itself is that it spreads quickly and widely. The printing press made a wide distribution of ideas possible. Movable letters made printing cheaper. From the end of the 15th century onward, ideas traveled across the European continent at an accelerating speed. From then on, invention and discovery went hand in hand with the rapid distribution of the new findings in science, technology, the arts, and their application in the production process.

Printing press and literacy led to the enlightenment and scientific revolution of the 17th century. The economic rise of Europe began as modern capitalism took shape. Leading the way was liberty, competition, and innovation along with reason, protecting the individual and of his property.

Capitalism came not by way of orders from the authorities but emerged from practical wants and needs as a spontaneous order. Modern capitalism blossomed where the private initiative could unfold.

The new type of the profit-seeking enterprise grew out of the world of the common people. The entrepreneurial pioneers at the dawn of the industrial revolution were artisans, traders, and engineers. These new leaders - the capitalist entrepreneurs - built the first industrial machines and invented mass products. They founded companies and became factory-owners - from Thomas Newcomen (1664-1729), the inventor of the steam engine (1712), Friedrich Krupp (1787-1826) in steel, and Werner von Siemens (1816-1892) in electricity, to Gottlieb Daimler (1834-1900) in the automobile, and to Thomas Edison (1847-1936), the inventor of the usable light bulb (1880).

Fundamentals of modern capitalism

The intellectual foundation of modern capitalism, which took shape in the two to three centuries before the industrial revolution, comprised the triad of the market, literacy, and the freedom of speech. Scientific thinking as a logical and experimental approach could, therefore, gain ground. The Enlightenment in the 18th century made independent thought and the artistic and scientific creativity its basic pillars.

Factors that laid the groundwork for modern capitalism

Political-spiritual factors

- individuality
- personal freedom
- rationality
- empiricism
- experimentation
- tolerance
- legality
- skepticism
- legality

Economic-material factors

- new sources of food
- increased supply of silver and gold
- printer with mobile letters
- global commerce
- accounting
- profit-oriented entrepreneurship

Besides the political-spiritual factors such as individuality, personal freedom, and more, economic-material factors laid the groundwork for the take-off of modern capitalism in Europe. Besides accounting and the emergence of companies and run by profit-oriented entrepreneurs, the discovery of America contributed through the access to new sources of food and the supply of silver and gold. The discovery of America also contributed to the intensification of global commerce.

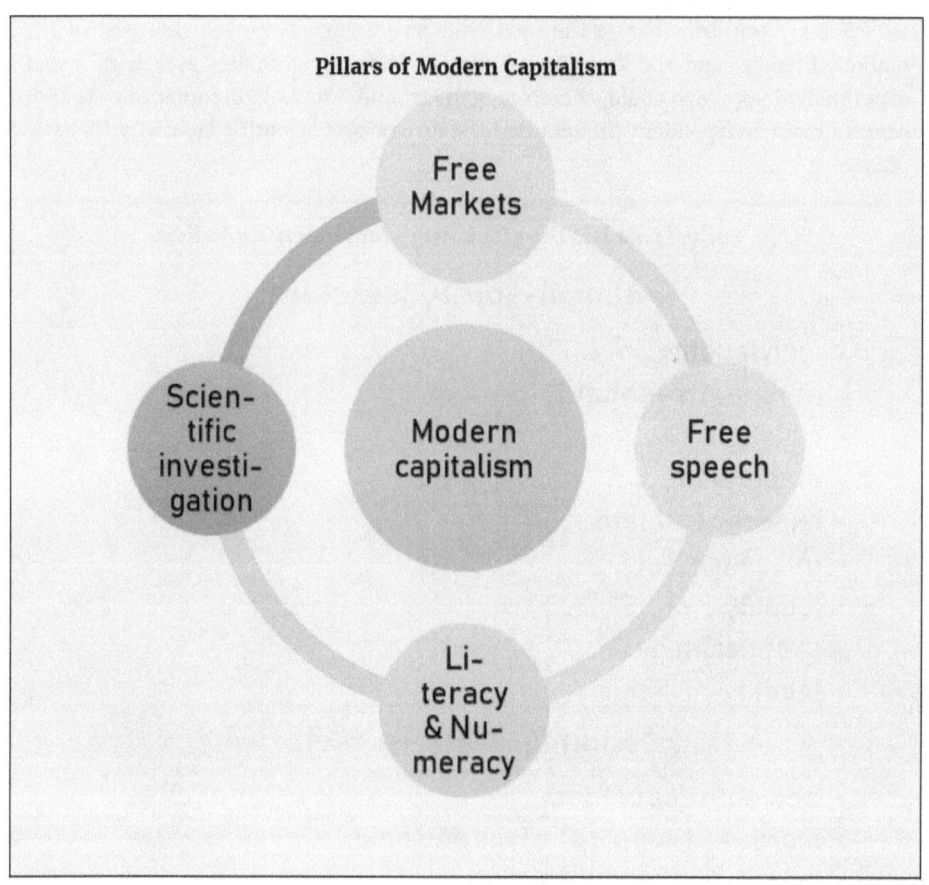

Pillars of Modern Capitalism

The entrepreneur is the motor of modern capitalism. The entrepreneurial task is to enforce innovations. In contrast to management and engineering knowledge, entrepreneurship is not a teachable subject because it is the opposite of routine, rules, and conventions. The entrepreneurial activity in capitalism consists in violating the standards, in abandoning the familiar and in bringing new things and new processes toward a breakthrough. Neither socialism nor feudalism or the ancient slave societies has a place for this person.

The discovery of gold and silver in America contributed to developing the monetary underpinnings of capitalism. Introducing double bookkeeping in Italy in the 15th century inspired modern mathematical thinking and provided business with the accounting tool to direct large enterprises. A network of payment and credit institutions spread across Europe. These developments happened spontaneously, locally and without a central power. As such, they were not the result of legislation but these individual areas, such as the foreign trade, developed their own legal principles, their own rules and their own ethics of business. Modern capitalism did not arise through the state, but it emerged and developed alongside the state as a parallel society.

MARKET PROCESS AND COMPETITION

Economic competition is not the same kind as competition is in sports. In sports, the goal - and thus the criterion of performance - is pre-determined. The competition is about to jump higher or farther, to run faster or to score more goals than the opponents. The 'end-product', so to speak, is given. In the market economy, however, competition is different. In economic competition what matters is to find out what the customers want and then to produce it at a favorable price. Contrary to sports with its rule-books, the machinations of economic competition are tacit and change with the competition process. The entrepreneurial behavior comprises advancement and imitation. For some time, a firm can earn excess profits by offering a product that more than that of the other vendors meets the tastes and wants of the customers. The economic game is about innovations, which change the rules, either in small steps by incremental advancements or by leaps due to major technological breakthroughs.

Successful projects find imitators. Imitation reduces the pioneers' profits and provides lower prices to the customers. As innovations diffuse over time throughout the economies and raise the economic productivity in all countries that take part in world trade, prosperity spreads around the globe.

Capitalism rests on special ownership of the means of production. The more intense competition, the more private property will serve the community. Competition functions as a control mechanism. The more competition prevails, the less it is necessary for the government to interfere with the property.

The more dynamic competition, the less the need for legal consumer protection.

Competition serves the public. The more there is economic competition, the less there is space for economic power. With a restricted market entry, private ownership loses its economic function. This was the case before the industrial revolution. The rulers granted monopolies to secure their power and gain a stream of income for themselves from the sale of the monopoly right. When the state grants such monopolies, property loses its capitalist meaning and becomes a domain. This economic system is far away from free capitalism.

Private ownership allows self-initiative and motivates one to manage the constant adjustment to the changing circumstances. Private ownership ensures the incentive to control costs and strive for innovation. Property rights, in their essence, begin with one's own person. A minimum state in this sense is thus always a state of law since it has the right of the individual as its first principle.

The value of a good is not an objective category. Value is individual and subjective according to the situation in which the individual finds himself with his needs and wants. The relative value of a good is not fixed but changes with the external and internal conditions. The economic actor must revalue the goods according to the current and expected circumstances and the changing personal needs and tastes. A meal has a different value, depending on whether one begins to eat the meal, or one has just ended eating a meal. It is therefore impermissible to infer from the overall benefit to the price, or even to justify the socialization of the production of certain goods because these are indispensable for human survival.

Backgrounder: Utility, value, and price

The utility is subjective and varies from person to person. Units of goods with objectively the same characteristics have different utilities for different persons. Universally, however, the law of decreasing marginal utility holds, which says that the more units of the same goods one consumes, the less is the marginal utility of each additional unit.

This 'saturation law', according to which, in an act of consumption, the respective following unit creates a diminishing limit value until the marginal utility disappears at the saturation point, was first formulated in 1854 by Hermann Heinrich Gossen (1810-1858).

Since the same good can serve in different ways and for different purposes, the utility of the good varies. Water, for example, can be used to drink, or to take a bath, or to wash one's car.

As a rule, the valuation of a good is given by the usefulness of the last unity of this good in the ranking of the available amount.

Eugen von Boehm-Bawerk (1851-1914) shows this principle by the example of Robinson Crusoe who has five sacks of grains of objectively the same quantity and quality but values each individual sack differently according to the urgency of his needs and ranks them accordingly.

In line with his subjective valuation, Robinson places at the first rank the unit which serves him to produce bread as his basic meal. The contents of the second sack of grain is to make cakes. The grain in the third sack serves to feed the chickens while the purpose of the grain in the fourth sack is to produce beverages and the fifth sack of grain is for his parrot as a pet.

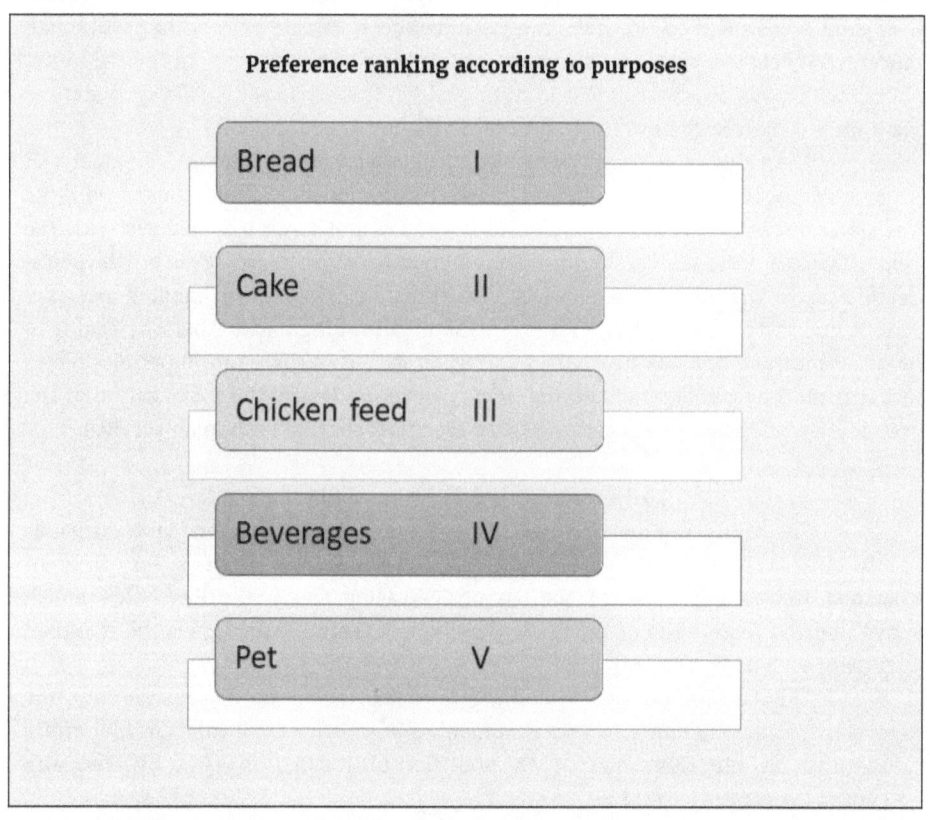

According to the marginal theory, the utility of the five sacks of grain depend on the value of the last sack on the ranking. The ranking is not as to the good but concerns the purpose of the use of the good. The ranking is an act of human valuation. The order of preference is not in the goods but in the mind of the acting person. It would be erroneous to assume that the grain in the first sack on the rank order because it serves the livelihood, had the greatest value. This consideration neglects that the contents of the bags are identical and therefore interchangeable.

For example, if the grain of the sack of grain that should provide the basic food is lost, the grain of the last sack serves to substitute it and is used for making bread. This may continue until the last bag. Accordingly, the availability of the last unit of the order of the rank, which the economic actor assigns to the same commodity units, determines the value of the individual units.

The willingness to pay a certain price for a good depends on the marginal utility of the last unit, and not on the average or the overall value of the good. Although water, for example, is necessary for human survival, the price per unit is low, so long as enough units are available to satisfy the many uses of water. As long as there is enough water to wash one's car, the price of water to drink will likewise be cheap.

The value of a meal is different whether one is hungry or full. A specific medicine, which is necessary for the survival of one person, is useless for the person without the ailment.

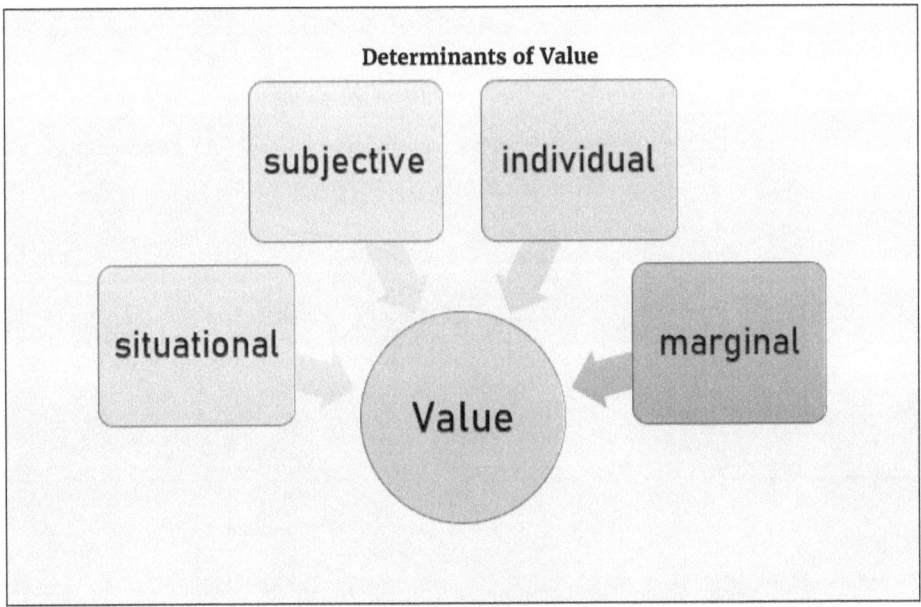

The same context applies to production. The opportunity costs determine the value of a production factor as to its contribution to producing a good. Value, therefore, depends on the extent to which its marginal contribution is substitutable. This explains, for example, why the wage for a professional activity does not depend on how difficult it is to acquire this ability, but to what extent the activity is substitutable for the current production process to produce a good of high demand.

The value a production factor, such as labor or capital, in its contribution to produce a good depends on its opportunity costs, that is, on the extent to which its marginal contribution is substitutable. This explains, for example, that the remuneration of an activity does not depend on how difficult or painful it is to acquire a skill but to what extent the activity is substitutable for the current production process or not, and whether customers will pay for this product.

Value determination and factor remuneration

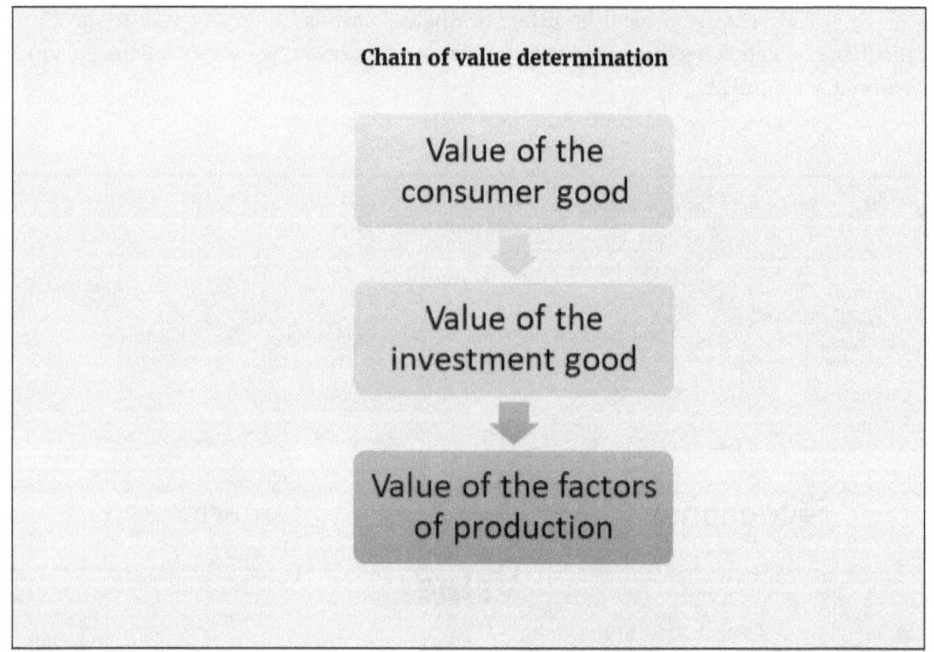

The value that the consumers contribute to the consumption good determines the value of the investment good. Not costs determine price, but the price that one can get for a consumption good determines the value of the investment good and consequently that of the factors of production.

The sale price of the consumer good provides the yardstick for the profitability of the investment and determines the remuneration of the factors of production in terms of wages and profits.

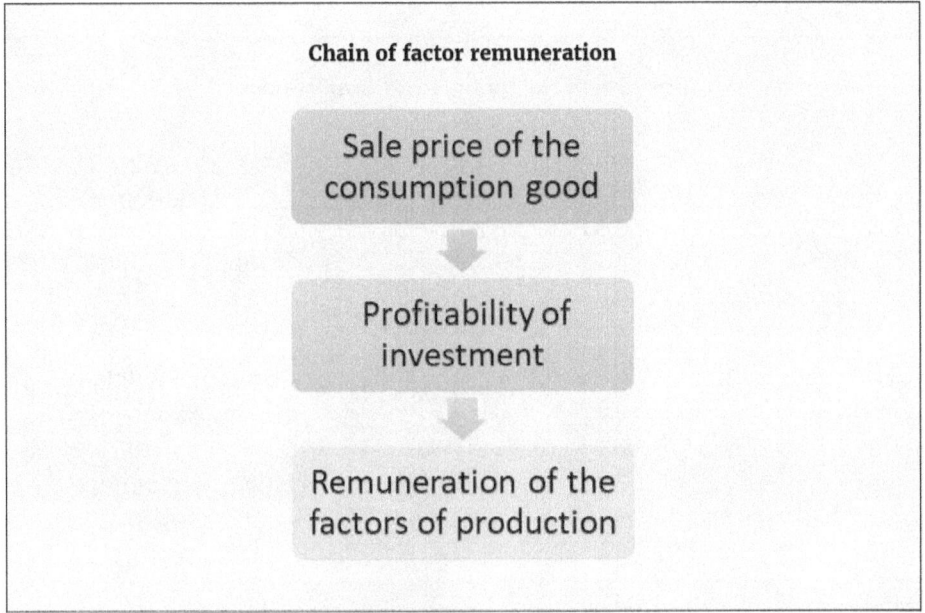

Prices and their function

Prices represent income for the seller and are costs for the buyer. Prices inform about income and costs. They provide incentives for the seller to sell more if prices rise and to cut sales when prices fall.

Different from the buyer, for whom prices are costs, the incentives of the price call for buying less when prices rise and buy more when they fall.

This way, the prices on free markets move toward an equilibrium although they may never reach the condition of equilibrium in the sense of 'rest' and 'stability'.

The price-driven market process unfolds in response to a higher demand with an increasing quantity offered due to higher prices. Rising profits in the product segment, where a demand increase takes place, induce the entry of new suppliers along with expanding the production by the established firms. Suppliers thus expand the offer and increase the companies' capacity to deliver.

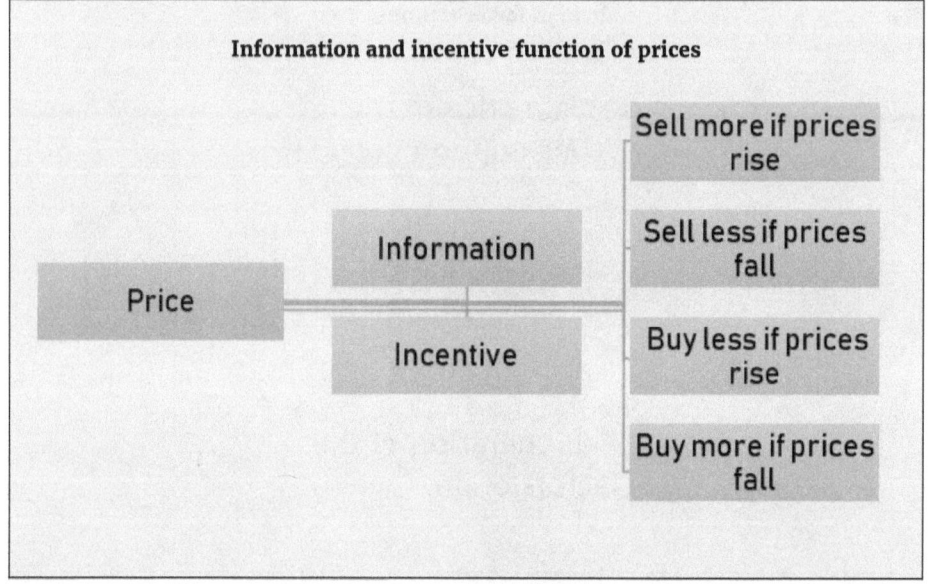

The market grows, and the prices fall. Lower prices lift the quantity demanded. The market enjoys a larger supply of goods at lower prices. A new market equilibrium takes hold.

To become effective, the price system must work properly, and this requires the absence of political interventions. When evaluating the market efficiency of concrete cases, one must keep in mind that already beginning with taxes, many political effects are at work that distort the system. It is wrong to assume perfect competition when capitalism is not free. The freer capitalism is, the more the markets will move to the ideal of perfect competition.

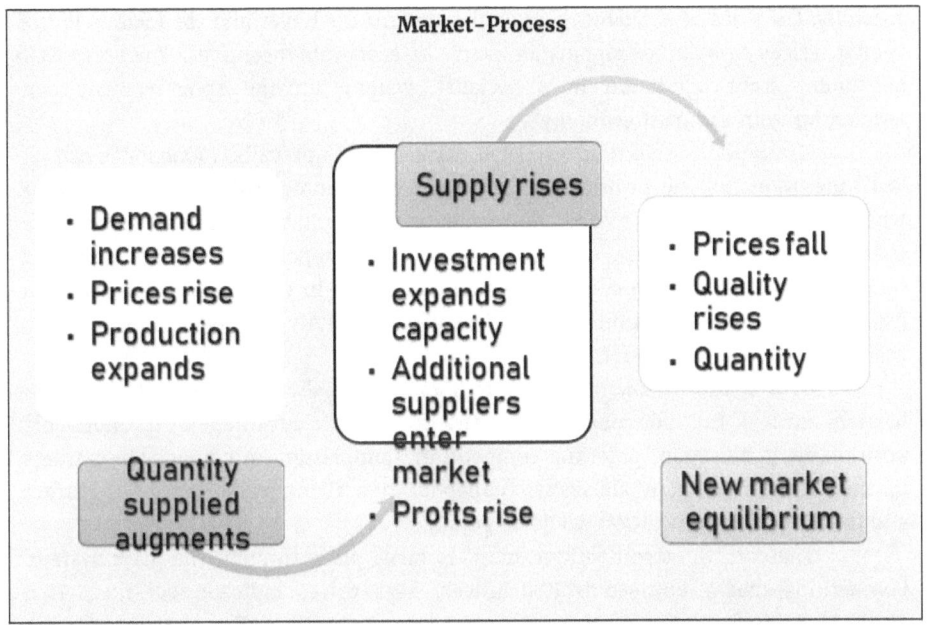

***

According to the individual assessment of benefits, the buyer determines his willingness to pay. In a market economy, all roads begin with the consumer. He is at the center of the system. His wishes and his preferences serve as input to shape the structure of the production apparatus. The demands of the consumers determine the value of the investment goods.

Entrepreneurs must act on behalf of the customer to earn a profit. The consumer as the end-user is the ultimate customer. The system works best when it can operate without distorting interferences. This is the meaning of the laissez-faire principle. A laissez-faire economy is an economy in which there is free space for the private initiative. The idea of 'laissez-faire' is not 'let it be' but rather 'let us do it'. As such, the saying refers to the role of entrepreneurs to satisfy the consumers' wishes without requiring state approval.

Once the legal system recognizes and guarantees the private ownership of the means of production, the market economy arises with the price system as its central facility.

Prices have two functions. They provide information on scarcity, and secondly, the price of a product signals the cost for the buyer and the income to the vendor. Prices function as signals and serve as economic incentives. The areas that are under state regulation in a socialist system, emerge spontaneously and automatically in a market economy.

If competition with unrestricted market access prevails, monopolies cannot last long. Monopolistic positions on the basis of technological progress disappear when further innovation makes the former obsolete. Stable monopolies require a charter by the state. Pure capitalism is not a monopoly capitalism. Monopoly capitalism is the consequence of crony capitalism. As in feudalism, such a system leads to economic stagnation and to a loss of productivity because the incentive to cost control and to innovation is lost.

In a market economy, even if a monopoly should exist, but the entry barriers are low, the monopolistic company cannot take advantage of its monopoly position, as it must face potential competition. Competition in contestable markets means that if a company abuses its monopoly, new firms would enter the market and the monopolistic position would be gone.

The control of competitive markets takes place through the price system. Competition means auto-control. Relatively high prices indicate that there is a scarcity of this good. Since prices represent income for the seller and costs for the buyer, there is an automatism on competitive markets, which leads to the alleviation of the scarcity. The producers will supply more goods when the price rises whereas the buyers of this commodity will demand less and use the product more economically when it becomes expensive. In order to function this way, the property must be private, and the costs must be borne by the individual owner.

In a free competition, there is a tendency to equilibrium on the market, which corresponds to the best use of the resources. This condition, however, is only temporary, since neither the wishes of the consumers nor the technology remains constant.

Higher relative prices show that there is inadequate production in relation to the demand for this product. In the first phase, this will lead to better utilization of existing production facilities. There is an increase in the quantity offered. In the second phase, there will be an increase in the supply when investments have enlarged the production capacity.

The signaling and incentive mechanisms of the price system on competitive markets provide the conditions that suppliers and demanders adapt their behavior according to price changes in the area where there is a discrepancy between demand

and supply. The interplay of supply and demand thus ensures, by means of entrepreneurial action, that capital flows into such areas where demand is high relative to the supply, while entrepreneurs remove capital from areas where there is an abundance of capital and where overcapacity exists. This is the basic principle of the allocative efficiency of the market economy.

It is a boon and a tragedy that even with severe interventions, the price system works well. While the price system is robust enough to support many interventions, it is not immune and invulnerable. Each individual intervention weakens the market so that the quality of its performance decreases. With each intervention, the malfunctions accumulate. The capacity of markets to adapt slows down. It takes longer for the supply to respond to demand shifts. Gaps widen between supply and demand. It is as much paradoxical as it is tragic that these gaps, which result from excessive intervention, serve the interventionist to demand more interventions. The result is the interventionist spiral which says that each interference will lead to new additional interventions because the interference before has deteriorated the market performance, to begin with.

The efficient allocation of capital means that capital flows into those areas where it yields the highest returns. Because of this shift in the capital structure, the bottlenecks of supply disappear, and excess profits vanish. The faster and the more capital flows into the area where most of the scarcity prevails, quicker the bottlenecks vanish and the faster extraordinary capital gains dissolve.

It is the essence of the market economy that special profits arise and that because of that, individual companies and their owners accumulate wealth. At the same time, however, the market system functions in such a way that, when the allocation process can go on unhampered, extra profits disappear. The more dynamic the economy is in the sense that there are open markets and that entrepreneurial action has great leeway, the less is there a persistent deficiency of supply. The more capitalist the economy, the faster extra profits dissipate.

Interventionist spiral

The price system does not always work to perfection. The criticism of the 'market failure', however, misses the crucial point because in the real world it does not so much matter whether markets are perfect but how robust the price system works and whether even under unfavorable conditions it is still functioning to indicate scarcity.

Some interventionists conclude that the market economy is indestructible and that one can intervene as much as one wants. This view is as erroneous as the theory of market failure that uses perfection as the criterion. Errors as these, form the intellectual basis of the interventionist spiral. A perceived, yet de facto non-existent, market failure leads to market intervention whereby this interference into the market produces the market failure the interventionist claims to cure when in fact it was the interference that brought the failure into existence. This way, the interventionist receives the confirmation of his claim and he will go on with further interventions although it was the market intervention itself that provoked the apparent 'market failure'.

PRICES AND COMPETITION

The price of a good or service results from the interplay of supply and demand and the estimation of the commodity's utility by the individual market participants. Pricing in competitive markets means that the market price tends towards the minimum average costs where it equals marginal costs. The interplay of demand and supply is in constant change and relative prices move according to the relative degrees of scarcity. The market equilibrium balances the quantity demanded with the quantity offered. The law of supply and demand says that the higher the price, the higher the quantity offered and the lower the quantity demanded.

The interplay between supply and demand, on the one hand, and, on the other hand, the subjective utility and the opportunity costs, determine the price. The utility estimate of the individual market participant determines the individual value of the goods. The value of a good is not equal to its price.

While the price is an objective category, its value is subjective. The determinants of the value are subjective, individual, and situational. The value estimation changes marginally depending on the situation in which the individual operates. Scarcity means that goods are less available than people want. As determinants of prices (not as an accounting tool) costs are opportunity costs and, in this sense, as subjective as the utility.

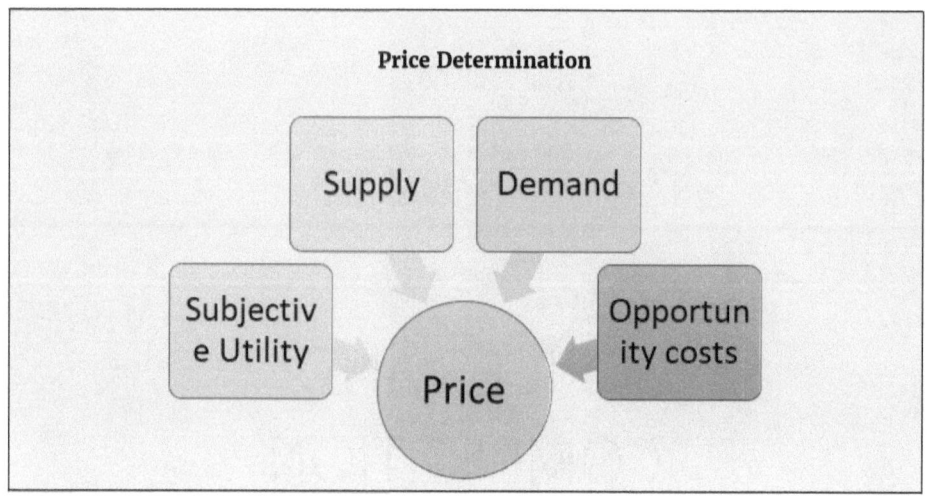

Scarcity is not an objective, but a subjective category. For a good to be scarce, it is not sufficient to be just rare. Scarcity describes the relation between the supply of a specific good and a person's subjective valuation of this good. Thus, the same kind of meal is scarce for a person who is hungry, yet no longer scarce after the person has eaten and is full. The relative prices of goods are numerical market phenomena. They come about through the interaction of the market participants. The equilibrium rate indicates at which price the highest possible number of transactions takes place in a market. The dynamism of capitalist competition unfolds from innovations that lead to pioneering profits. This market dominance due to a new product or a new process is only temporary.

If there is a free market entry, competitors will try to mimic the new products and processes, thereby differentiating and improving innovation.

The temporary monopoly profits diminish with the additional offer on the market. A new market equilibrium is emerging.

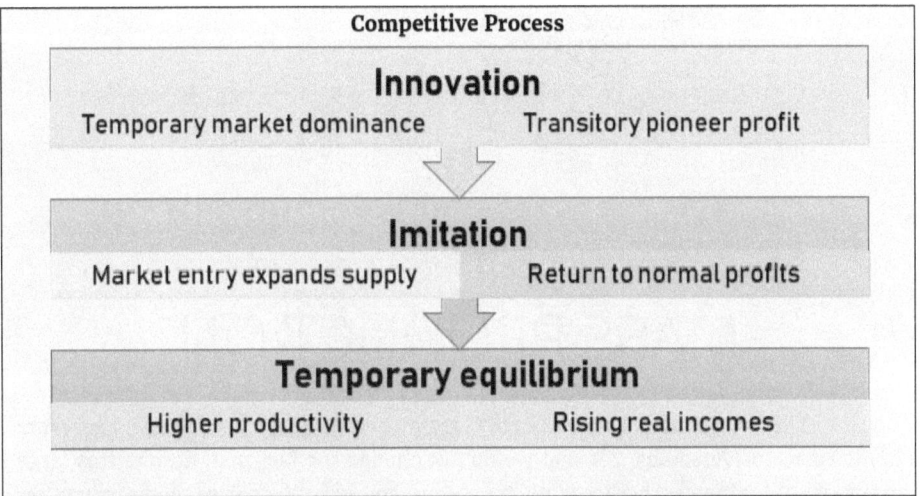

Product and process renewals spread across the market according to demand. At the pioneer company, profits go down to normal, while consumers' purchasing power and their real income increase to a higher level.

Antony P. Mueller

MASS PRODUCTION

The French king Louis XIV (1638-1715) had more than a thousand servants in his Palace of Versailles. Yet that would not change the fact that, despite this large group of subordinates, there was no hot water shower in the palace, and many other items of comfort were lacking, which nowadays are in every apartment of a social housing project. The sun king wore an impressive wig, and he was perfumed, yet this was necessary because there was no shampoo and the equipment of the palace with 'toilets' was well below any modern standards.

Before the industrial revolution, the rich were poorer than the poor today in the capitalist industrialized countries. Nowadays, the common tourist travels to Versailles by coach or by car. When he has finished his sightseeing, thousands of waiters and other servants in thousands of restaurants, cafes, bars, and hotels are waiting in Paris to entertain this tourist with food, drink, and bed.

Modern capitalism serves the mass of the consumers. Those who work in the factories are the same people who consume the goods, which are manufactured there.

The equipment of US households with durable consumer goods such as telephone, electricity, automobile, radio, refrigerator, cooker, washing machine, tumble dryer, color-TV, air conditioning, dishwasher, microwave, video player, computer, mobile phones, and the Internet.

The process of spreading the consumer goods among the population is speeding up. While it took more than half a century for the phone and the car to reach over 80% of the households, it only took a decade for the video players and the mobile phones.

What is remarkable about this process is that many of the modern consumer goods not only make life easier and more enjoyable, such as a microwave oven or the access to hot water, but the modern goods also increase the value of leisure, such as the radio, television, video games, and the Internet.

HOW CAPITALISM CREATES WEALTH & PROMOTES PROSPERITY

***

Prosperity finds its expression not only in more consumption but also in the access to a better quality of goods and to a greater variety of products. Nowadays, a medium-sized supermarket runs an assortment that goes into the tens of thousands of different products.

The difference between the past and the present shows up in the general life expectancy. Two hundred years ago, average life expectancy was under forty years. In the meantime, life expectancy has doubled, and the average purchasing power has risen by a multiple. Compared to the past, not only the quantity of the goods has increased but likewise their quality and even more so the variety of goods.

Life expectancy has increased since 1800. Before the industrial revolution, life expectancy was around 30 years in all regions of the world. Since 1800, the global average life expectancy has more than doubled and is now around 70 years on average and over 80 years in some advanced countries.

Life expectancy has not only increased because of a falling child mortality. In 1841, a 5-year-old could expect to live 55 years. Today a 5-year-old can expect to live 82 years. At higher ages, mortality patterns have also changed, so that compared to the time before the industrial revolution, the life expectancy of a 50-year-old has increased from 20 years to 33 years. (Max Roser, Our World in Data. Life Expectancy. https://ourworldindata.org/life-expectancy/)

***

Economic growth is a false term if it denotes bigger and more. Growth in capitalism consists in using new, better, and cheaper goods. The basis of economic growth is higher productivity and technical progress in all its variants. In the course of this development, more people are enjoying goods, which were accessible only to the rich. No other economic system has brought as much prosperity to ordinary people than modern capitalism. This economic system creates new wealth through the ongoing process of 'creative destruction'. Technological progress is the motor of the entrepreneurial monetary economy, and production for the masses is its hallmark. The capitalist system promotes adaptable and efficient firms and eliminates the less productive enterprises. The basic conflict of modern capitalism does not consist in the struggle of capitalists against proletarians but in the conflict between pioneers and laggards, between those who produce change and adapt to change, and those who fall behind because they fail to change and to innovate. The conflict is between losers and winners, and workers and capitalists are found in both categories.

Corporate management is a constant endeavor for the highest possible productivity. Those companies will win the market competition that fulfill the wishes of the customer faster, better, and more cost-efficient than their competitors. In the long term, the rise of productivity will benefit everyone and reach the masses. The benefit comes at different times to different people. In the short term, there are losers in a relative way. Yet in the long run, capitalism makes everyone a winner.

Impatience is the enemy of economic growth. By redistribution, people want more goods now through political means even if they would get them through the natural process of economic growth in greater abundance later. People seldom notice that the market interventions, which they demand and the distributive benefits, which they receive, do not speed up to provide the goods but prolong the time of delivery because these measures slow down the dynamics of capitalism and because of these measures, productivity rises slower. The greatest enemy of the poor is redistribution because it keeps the poor in lethargic dependence.

Capitalism is a dynamic system. Uncertainty and risk are the prices of progress. Yet in this respect, the past was no different. On the contrary. Much more than today, people had to confront diseases, the weather, and the fluctuations of food production. A life of hunger, poverty, and misery marked most of the humankind before the industrial revolution. While there is never and nowhere a system of complete security in this world, free capitalism ends absolute poverty and makes the way free for individual success irrespective of one's origin. Need and care are the eternal companions of human existence. Even free capitalism does not lead to a carefree life. Yet capitalism liberates humankind from absolute misery and bondage.

In the pre-capitalist period, the inequality of wealth was greater than today. It is true that capitalism as an entrepreneurial monetary economy leads to accumulating wealth and income in some hands, but these extremes are now rather less than they were in the past, and above all, the relative wealth positions are not permanent in capitalism.

Since 1820, the world has become both richer and more equal. This development occurred because more countries have been moving to a capitalist economic order over the past 200 years. Max Roser: What on Earth is going on? https://ourworldindata.org/income-inequality/

Before the industrial revolution, the upper class was small. Much of the population lived in extreme poverty and need. Since then, poverty has declined in those regions, which have adopted and developed the system of entrepreneurial monetary capitalism. Earlier economic systems made a few persons rich, but the rest remained poor. Capitalism makes a few persons extremely rich, but it makes also the rest wealthier than in any other system.

Capitalism makes not only some people rich but also the rest much more prosperous than it has ever been in history.

***

The value of an investment project depends on the extent to which it contributes to satisfying the subjective individual utilities of the final consumers. The cost calculation is an indispensable tool to assess the profit chances of a project. The final judgment on the profits, however, is in the hands of the consumer. This also applies to investment goods, which have value as intermediate goods in so far as they contribute to the producing the consumer goods as the final goods. The individual additions to the value at each step along the stages of production receive their compensation when the final consumer pays for the goods.

The management of a company must fulfill the functions to estimate the future demand of the buyer and to produce the goods at the minimum cost. The attainment of these objectives requires experimentation to succeed. Business is trial and error. One can plan the trial but not its success. Competition serves to find out what consumers want and how to manufacture the goods in the most cost-effective way.

Modern capitalism serves the people through mass production and provides goods for mass consumption. In capitalism, there is no end to this process because the economy will grow with the pace of productivity. In order to understand this connection, one must keep in mind that in a competitive economy, economic profits result from higher productivity. In a market economy, economic growth is linked to profits, and profits result from productivity gains.

Main Features of Modern Capitalism

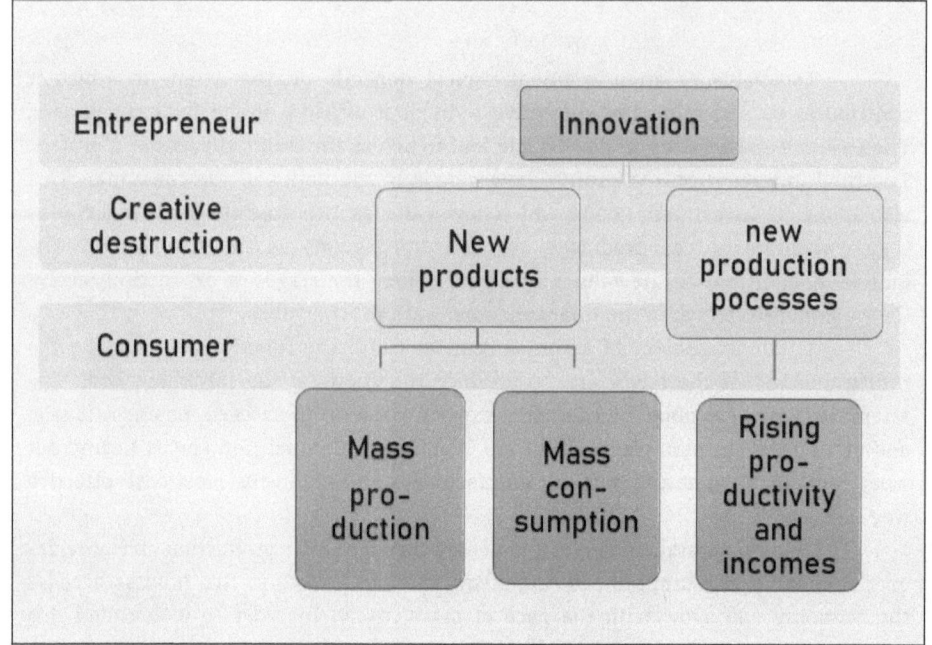

The function of the entrepreneur is to implement innovations.

The entrepreneur fulfills the task of creative destruction by overcoming the resistance against new products and new processes.

Different from the inventor or administrator, the entrepreneur is the one who has the specific ability to bring new products and new production methods to the market.

Innovation involves creative destruction as it breaks the prevailing market conditions and makes existing products and production processes obsolete.

Innovation benefits the consumers in the form of mass production and mass consumption, and due to higher productivity brings rising incomes and an increase of the purchasing power.

***

Capitalism means permanent revolution. In the market economy, there is no standstill and no equilibrium. New companies enter the scene; established companies disappear. Entrepreneurial activity creates new goods and modifies existing goods while obsolete products disappear from the market just as it happens with old production methods. Because of this dynamism, the structure of the market economy is changing and what was the case yesterday is no longer valid today. This means that new opportunities surface for new rivals to enter the market. In the market economy, the cards are re-distributed again and again. Crises are windows of opportunity when the asset prices fall. These crises offer chances for new companies with new projects. Instead of lamenting the crises, one should take them as a signal of the phases of economic transformation.

Capitalism is not perfect, but there is no other economic system where the advantages so outweigh the disadvantages. The capitalist economic system benefits above all the broad mass of the population. Capitalism delivers the goods, which at first were available only for the wealthy, to ever more people. Capitalism produces not only masses of goods but also more so new and improved goods.

Antony P. Mueller

FREEDOM AND CAPITALISM

Modern capitalism originated in Europe. Its cornerstones are commerce, cooperative competition, and decentralization along with private ownership of the means of production and the cultural ingredients such as individual dignity, love of truth, literacy, experimental (scientific) thinking, bookkeeping, and arithmetic. This modern capitalism experiences its legitimacy through the prosperity that it spreads. This prosperity is beneficial to the masses. Inequality exists, but under capitalism, inequality has an economic function; it serves as an incentive to achieve economic progress, i.e., to realize innovation and promote inventions.

The price system of the market economy ensures that supply and demand adapt to the conditions of scarcity. In this sense, there are no limits to growth. The scarcer a commodity, the more expensive it is on the market and the higher are the incentives to find substitutes and economize its use. Economic progress in capitalism results from constant efforts to produce goods of better quality at lower prices. The hallmark of entrepreneurial capitalism is the constant pressure to innovate.

The tendency to innovation, which is inherent in capitalism, provokes social change. These social commotions that come with capitalism call the anti-capitalists to the scene. In the resistance to accepting change as the essence of this economic system, modern history unfolds as a grand conflict. Since its emergence, modern capitalism must confront two separate opponents: Communism, born of utopian thought, and conservatism with its roots in the past. Communism and conservatism both continue to live on as great illusions. The socialist paradise does not come, and there is no way to go back in time.

In the market economy, every market participant pursues his own interest and promotes the common good because capital moves into those areas where scarcity is the highest. The consumer wants to increase his utility while the company's aim is to make profits. The universal language of the market is money in its expression as prices, costs, and profits. With the help of money prices, one can compare the goods with one another and relate the prices to one's income. The individual consumer can compare each good with every other good and weigh their price and value according to his personal preferences. This process happens also in production where the investment goods receive their valuation according to the extent to which they contribute to the profit of a company.

The monetary system, and thus the system of money-prices, does not function without error, but economic calculation without money is not possible when the process of production exceeds simple forms. In a household or in a small homestead, each associate can supervise all other members without the help of monetary calculation. Yet when the economic activities become more complex, one needs money and price calculation. Even that the purchasing value of money does not remain constant, does not outweigh the disadvantages of non-monetary management. Capital, for example, exists as a collection of production goods, but only its expression in monetary units makes it possible to speak of capital in terms of an entity and to relate it to other numbers, such as the yield, for example.

SUMMARY

There is no perfect economic system. Scarcity does not disappear. The earthly human life is limited in time, and time is the ultimate scarce resource of human existence. The necessity to evaluate trade-offs will persist. Yet capitalism fulfills its function of providing prosperity and freedom. Capitalism removes absolute poverty from the life of the masses. We are not at the end of capitalism but still at its beginning. There is still a long way to free capitalism. In order to improve this system, fundamental reforms of the financial system, of politics, and of the legal system are necessary. More capitalism does not mean disorder. On the contrary. The freer the economy, the higher the productivity and thus the income. Rising income means less poverty. This is the great achievement of modern capitalism. Since the industrial revolution over two hundred years ago, the percentage of people living in poverty has declined worldwide. This development has come about because more countries have dropped their feudal and socialist regimes in favor of capitalism.

That the future belongs to capitalism must be understood in such a way that the future belongs to those countries, which put the least obstacles into place against the development of a free economy. It should be clear to everyone that if Europe or America will not do it, other countries and regions are already on the way to a free capitalism.

II.
THE POLITICS AND ECONOMICS OF WEALTH CREATION

Antony P. Mueller

"INNOVATION IS THE OUTSTANDING FACT IN THE ECONOMIC HISTORY OF CAPITALIST SOCIETY OR IN WHAT IS PURELY ECONOMIC IN THIS HISTORY, AND IT IS ALSO LARGELY RESPONSIBLE FOR MOST OF WHAT WE WOULD AT FIRST GLANCE TRACE TO OTHER FACTORS."

JOSEPH SCHUMPETER: BUSINESS CYCLES: A THEORETICAL, HISTORICAL, AND STATISTICAL ANALYSIS OF THE,CAPITALIST PROCESS 1939 (NEW YORK: MCGRAW-HILL), P. 86

- *The meaning of economic growth -*
- *Growth traps -*
- *Backgrounder: The rise and fall of parasitic economies -*
- *Economics of wealth creation -*
- *Backgrounder: time preference -*
- *Backgrounder: Interest, consumption, and savings -*
- *Value creation and capital structure -*
- *The state as an enemy of growth -*
- *Creative destruction -*
- *Obstacles to innovation -*
- *Free trade -*
- *Summary*

Productivity is the key to prosperity. Without productivity gains, there is no rise in incomes. Escaping from poverty requires economic growth. Yet what brings about economic growth? The term 'growth', when applied to the economy, is misleading. Although economic growth means a higher production and a higher per capita income of the population, it is that the economy must not only grow bigger, but it must become more productive. If one were to produce always more with the same methods of production as in the past without technical progress, the economy would reach the limits of growth. The key to understanding economic growth is productivity.

In capitalism, there are no limits to growth because innovation is the motor of economic change. Because of the technological progress, the economy becomes more productive. When productivity rises, it takes less input to produce the same amount of output or with the same amount of input one can produce a higher output.

The price system tackles the problem of scarcity. If certain resources become scarcer, their price will rise in a free market economy. The self-interest of consumers and producers leads them to use the scarce goods more carefully and to look for a replacement. The higher the relative price for an existing product, the more rewarding is it to change to its substitute.

THE MEANING OF ECONOMIC GROWTH

Economic growth in terms of a rise in per capita income is a child of the industrial revolution. The passage toward rising productivity came because of companies that systematically put a part of their profits back into expanding their businesses. This principle still holds today. In a country where the population is still too poor to save enough, it is up to the companies to finance investment from their own profits. England has shown this path during its leadership of the industrial revolution. The other countries, which have industrialized, have followed this model. The economic recoveries of Germany and Japan after World War II used this method. China's development policy uses re-investing profits as the main means of funding investment. Countries failed in economic growth where the state installed monopolies where the profitability of the companies remained suppressed or where – because of the danger of expropriation – the reinvestment of profit has been too risky and the outcomes too uncertain. In principle, capital accumulation has failed where investment was not in private hands but largely in the hands of state companies.

Types of savings

One must distinguish between private and public savings. Public savings refer to the balance of the government's receipts in relation to its spending. Having a budget deficit means that public saving is negative. As such, it will diminish the level of national savings. Private savings comprise the savings of families and businesses. Net savings of families takes place when consumption is lower than income. Reinvested profits by companies count as savings. Savings in the form of reinvested profits foster economic growth because it allows the funding new ventures with one's own financial means.

The gross domestic product (GDP) is the sum of the production of the individual companies of a country's private and public companies. Not 'the' national economy produces the GDP, but the national product is the output of the multitude of a country's private and public firms. In order to achieve a higher total product, the factories, offices, and the other production units that sell their products on the market must produce more. Economic growth happens at the level of the individual companies. The growth dynamics of an economy depends on the constellation of factors that determine the incentives for companies to produce more or whether the entrepreneurial creation of value confronts obstacles that inhibit and block wealth accumulation. In so far as the public expenditures depend on taxation, all economic growth rests on the shoulders of the productivity of a country's companies.

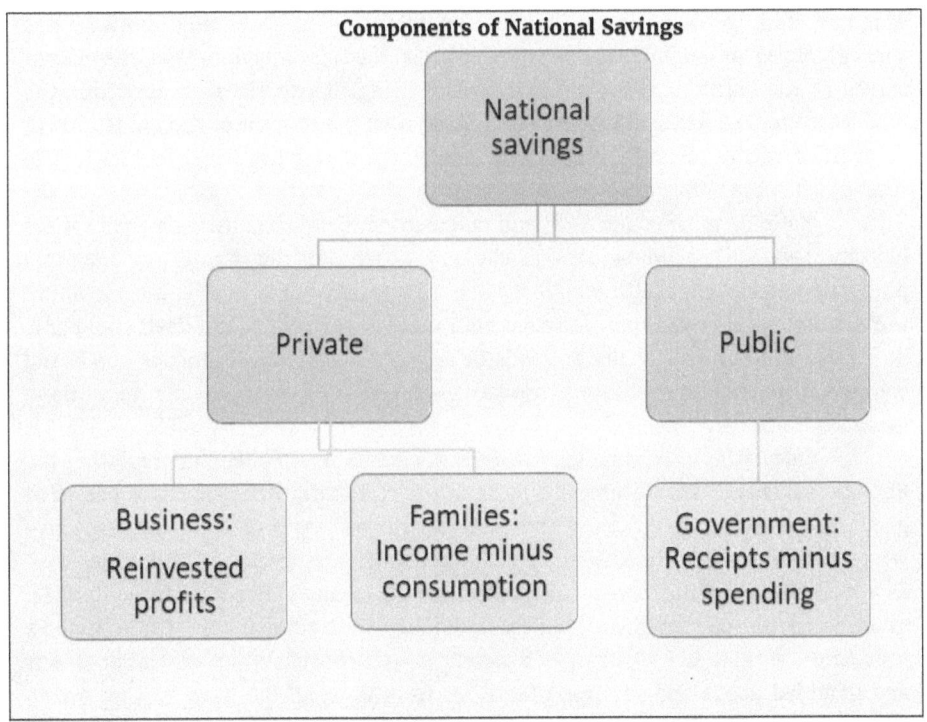

Economic growth serves as the prominent standard for measuring the performance of an economy. However, what gets published as the gross domestic product (GDP) does not represent production but reports overall spending.

Calculating economic growth is based on the nominal gross domestic product deflated by a price index.

The figure for economic growth is subject to two distortions: the indicator does not measure production but reports expenditures, and, second, the number for 'real gross domestic product' depends on the techniques to calculate the price index.

Economic growth figures can be determined fairly accurate for an economy, which is in a primitive state when a few identifiable and compoundable items are being produced, as it is the case with basic agricultural products. In the 1950s and 1960s, one used also tons of steel, for example, as a proxy for a timely estimate of a country's economic performance. Nowadays, the figure for the gross domestic production gets all the attention, although the basis for its calculation is more fragile than before.

Economic growth had its heyday with the spread of the social gospel that it is up to the state and its government to guarantee general welfare by managing the economy and to redistribute income. In this context, economic growth was conceptualized as an increase in standardized goods production, and the output served as the benchmark for the standard of living. It was for such aims that the modern system of national income accounting with the concept of economic growth at its heart was established, and this measurement device has never lost its link to mass production.

National income statistics and macroeconomic models use as a premise the identity between spending and production based on the tautology that sold production equals expenditures. What is being calculated here is this: income and – as its tautological counterpart – spending. However, the production itself could only be measured in uniform units of goods or services. When heterogeneous goods and complex services get produced, overall aggregation is not possible in a non-monetary form.

Calculating economic growth in terms of 'real GDP' requires deflating the nominal values of expenditures. To do that, the statistical offices create a basket of goods and compare the prices of the goods in this basket to those of the respective reference periods. But there is no objective representative basket of GDP other than as a statistical construct constructed with the help of many disputable assumptions. There is no common standard, which would allow the comparison of one period's production to the other when in fact current output consists in an ensemble of new and modified goods and services that differ from those of the past. Neither for an individual nor a family or a nation, the 'basket of purchases' stays constant. It changes from day to day, and from months to months, not to speak of years and decades. There is no way how a statistical office or any other agency could trace all these changes.

Measuring the economy as a whole as it is the aim the GDP-figure owes its popularity to the Cold War and that its origins have their roots in managing the war economy of the first half of the 20th century. Before World War I, economists worked in a tradition that was for peace, free trade, and for limited government. Thereafter, the perspective changed. With the experience of the industrialized warfare machinery and of the welfare state, economists found a new expanding field of job opportunities for them in government activism. Consequently, the dominant philosophy of the discipline changed from laissez-faire to interventionism. It was in this context that the statistical and aggregate approach to economic issues gained its momentum.

The managers of a war economy want to measure output and its growth because the economy is at the service of the war aims. Then, the central planning authority can know whether the goods and services that it needs get produced and at which proportions the factors of production it should allocate. In a war economy, the distribution of the production is in the hand of the government. Under such conditions, the planners rank the increase in output, and economic growth, as it is measured as an increase in output, serves as the indicator of economic performance. For a private economy, this procedure makes no sense because only individual goals count, different from the 'collective purpose' of winning a war.

The more we move away from basic goods, and that we have an advanced and dynamic, non-stationary economy, with many heterogeneous goods and services, attempts to measure 'the economy' have become more complicated, and these calculations have lost much of their economic meaning. The concept of total output and its measurement and thus of economic growth is a statistical construct that lacks informational value for an economy characterized by a wide variety of goods and services and in which producing new types of goods and services occurs while many other items become obsolete.

The economy is not like a pumpkin that grows to maturity and whose size can be measured at each stage and whose weight can be compared from one season to the next. Also, the economy is not a cake we all bake and then consume together. It is this pumpkin-like and cake-like understanding of economic activity that has provided the basis for most of the popular fallacies regarding production, distribution, and economic policy-making.

For governments, using the figure of the GDP as an indicator of economic performance has contributed to severe illusions of fiscal and monetary policy such as when spending for consumption is said to produce wealth or when government spending should boost economic growth as it happens – among others – with military expenditures.

Times of war and the preparation for it come along with high economic growth rates. Festive state acts produce peaks of production. Likewise, GDP got a boost after a pharaoh had died in ancient Egypt and the economy under the order to build a new pyramid. Yet this growth has no benefit for the people. On the contrary.

The problem with economic growth goes beyond statistics. Approaching the economic problem in terms of growth and stability is a severe obstacle to understanding the true nature of the economic activity as an exchange-oriented action directed at improving personal conditions. Economic growth as measured by the gross domestic product directs the policymakers to the lump sum of an imaginary output instead of allowing a market-driven adaptation to the diverse needs, wants, and wishes of the individuals.

In the context of a non-collectivist economic theory, economic growth, as it is measured by real GDP, has no place. Likewise, in a non-collectivist economic system, the focus would be not on economic growth, but on the conditions of market exchange as the way to economic amelioration. Given that the criteria for assessing economic improvement are individual and subject to change, no guideline is adequate other than that there are unhampered markets, protection of property rights, and the freedom of private initiative.

In a non-collectivist economic system, the focus would not be on 'sustained economic growth' as the oxymoronic expression says for the 'common good' in economic policy. The individualistic economic theory would focus on the prevalent conditions of market exchange as the way to economic amelioration. In this view, what brings about improvement, comes not from economic growth or from stability, but through the economic transformation under the guidance of entrepreneurial action within an open market system.

The grand-scale interventions that monetary and fiscal policy perform in the name of growth and stability disrupt and misguide the plans of the individual economic actor. They distort the decisions at the business level. Applying macroeconomic growth models has caused havoc when economic leaders adopt the interventionist creed and believe that it just takes the handling of a few economic policy variables – like easy money or government expenditures – to achieve the blissful state of economic plenty.

Instead of its fixation on economic growth and stability, a non-interventionist system would favor leeway for individual decision-making to pursue his own preferences. The interventionist system, in contrast, puts the individual under serfdom where 'output' or rather 'expenditure' become the criteria. Economic growth puts a criterion of performance upon the individual that is detrimental to change and adaptation and to the individual pursuit of benefit. Not unlike the slave masters of the past, the modern interventionist state uses its levers to push the individual by incentives and constraints towards an obscure output that is called 'economic growth'.

GROWTH TRAPS

The productivity of human labor rises when more capital becomes available and when this capital finds productive use. Total factor productivity signifies an increase of output without an increase in labor and capital or other factors of production. Labor productivity – which determines the wage level – increases with capital accumulation, which requires investments and thus savings. The poverty trap comprises the vicious circle that savings will be low when income is low. Low-income per capita implies low savings per capita, and low savings per capita imply low investment. Because the capital stock does not grow, income per capita remains low. How can one save enough if the income is meager? This is the poverty trap, which had kept humankind in deprivation until the industrial revolution. Saving requires an income above the subsistence level. Yet to have a high per capita income one must accumulate capital first. This requires saving, which, in turn, depends on the income available.

The poverty trap consists in the vicious circle that low income allows only a low level of savings, and therefore of small investment. A low level of capital formation implies little production and income. If the investment is small, capital accumulation is also weak. A low level of capital goods means that income is also low. So long as there are no companies that earn and reinvest profits, there is no escape from the poverty trap.

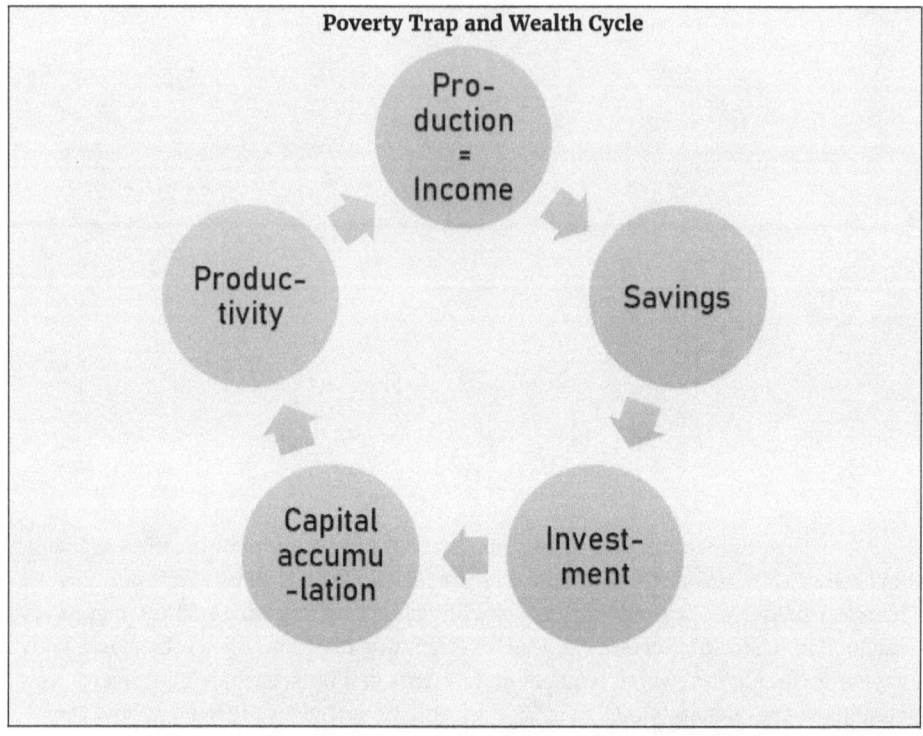

The poverty trap transforms into a wealth cycle when companies reinvest their profits. Capital formation in companies is the path to a higher production. The increase in productivity leads to higher incomes. When incomes rise, more savings are available and more capital formation and productivity gains become possible. The economy experiences its 'take-off'.

***

The violence trap aggravates the poverty trap. The world's history is a history of acts of violence because, throughout most of history, robbery was the preferred path to wealth. The state rose to historical prominence as a plundering machine. States represent the political means to gain a living different from the economical method. Every state is extractive in contrast to the economy, which is productive.

In the past, the great empires came into existence when one horde concentrated its efforts on martial purposes to prepare for the plundering of those groups that had settled to produce for consumption goods. Looting, however, works only until there is nothing left to loot. This way, all ancient empires were bound to fall.

HOW CAPITALISM CREATES WEALTH & PROMOTES PROSPERITY

As Franz Oppenheimer explains in his treatise on "The State" (German original "Der Staat" 1929), conquest and slavery have served as the means of exploitation throughout history. Plundering is a parasitic economy. When humans became sedentary, they dealt with nature no longer only in an extractive way, but productively as they began to plan crops and to cultivate domesticated animals and plants. Yet this did not put an end to poverty and violence. Robbery and oppression continued to gain a living when it came in the form of an organized state or as a state-like entity on a grand scale.

The problem of the parasitic economy is that parasites can survive only as a minority because their maintenance depends on the surplus product of the hosts. Yet the incentives structure that prevails in a parasitic economy provokes the proliferation of consumption by the parasites and a diminished production by the exploited part of the population. Therefore, parasitic wealth is not permanent.

The robber state disintegrates society. Raiding annihilates the incentive to accumulate capital and thus leads to a decline in productivity. The output of goods and services dwindles whereas the exigencies of the exploiters keep on rising. The basis of such parasitic societies erodes. In the end, the parasites perish together with their hosts.

Backgrounder:
The rise and fall of parasitic economies

Parasitic robber economies are not sustainable. They strengthen the parasites at the expense of the host in the first phase but lead in the second phase to the death of the host and thus of the parasite as well.

The more a country finds its way to prosperity, a more attractive victim it becomes for the parasites.

While the parasite grows through exploitation, the host gets weaker. The incentives in favor of parasitism are increasing while those for productive activity are shrinking.

The result is a decline of the host and the weakening of the parasite.

An economy based on robbery and parasitism is not sustainable. The capital stock decays, knowledge gets lost. In a parasitic state, distribution conflicts are always present and, therefore, the costs of production are high. Parasitic economies are inefficient.

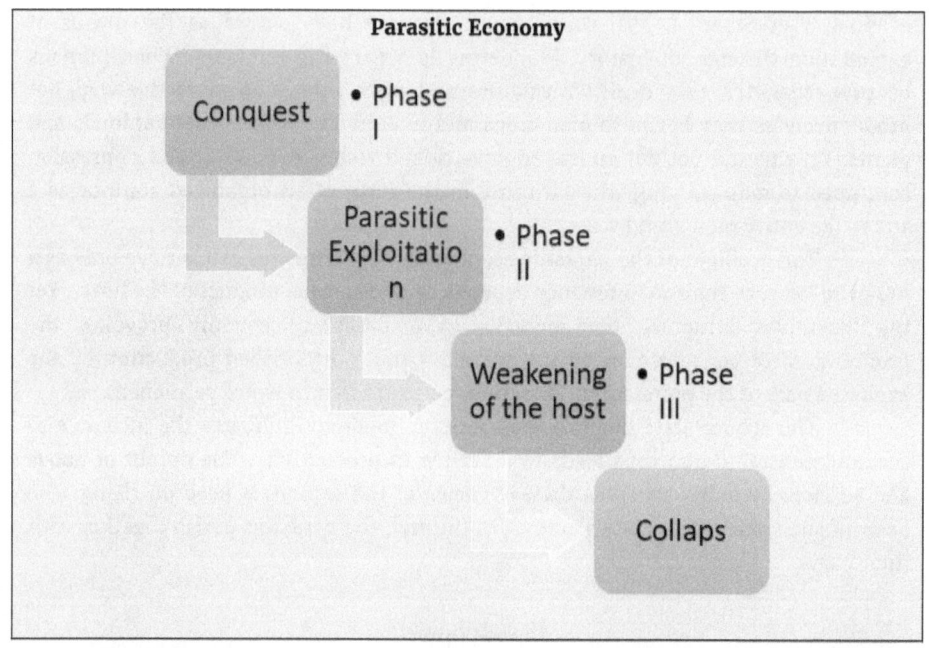

The exploitative economy and society arise through violence, maintains itself through violence, and disintegrates through violence. At the end of the process, both the host and the parasite will perish.

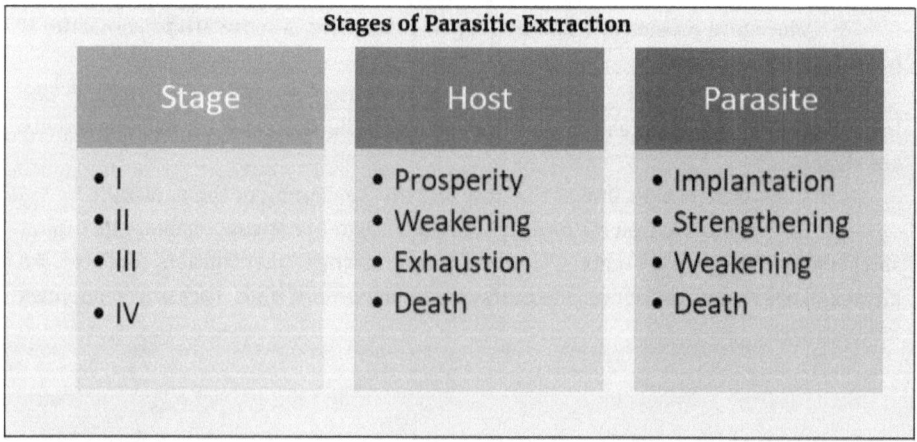

Modern societies suppress the private exertion of violence and arm themselves against robbery and violence from abroad, but this does not exclude institutionalized robbery by the state itself against its own citizens. While the state holds the monopoly of the use of force in modern societies, subtle ways of extraction have replaced the open exploitation of the empires of the past.

***

The history of humanity is a history of parasitic robber economies. Before the industrial revolution, a warlike orientation of a country's economy was superior to a society that focused on the peaceful production of consumption goods. Modern capitalism has changed this balance. Since modern capitalism has taken hold, those countries that have a consumer-oriented economy are also militarily strong. However, exploitation and violence have not ended. Today, while the wealth in the industrialized countries is less in danger from private violence and from foreign invasion, wealth creation is at risk from the state itself.

The state, whose original function was to protect property, has become its fiercest violator. Although property rights still enjoy recognition, these rights are under attack by the state itself, most prominently by taxation and other forms of redistribution. In a perverse twist of history, to achieve domestic peace and security against external attacks has not closed the doors to domestic parasitism. The modern parasitism hides behind the mask of social justice and equality.

Backgrounder: Population Growth and Income

Until the industrial revolution, humankind found itself in the demographic trap. As more food became available per capita, there were more offspring. With the rise of the population, the increase in food per capita would disappear.

It took until the industrial revolution around 1800 that technical progress accelerated so that the rate of food production exceeded that of human reproduction.

Before the industrial revolution, gains in production did not compensate for the increase of the population that came with a better provision of goods.

The rise of income per capita in the first phase such made the way to the fall of income per capita in the following phase.

Despite the sharp increase in the population since the start of the industrial revolution, there has been no food shortage in the capitalist countries except for wars or other conflicts.

Population Trap

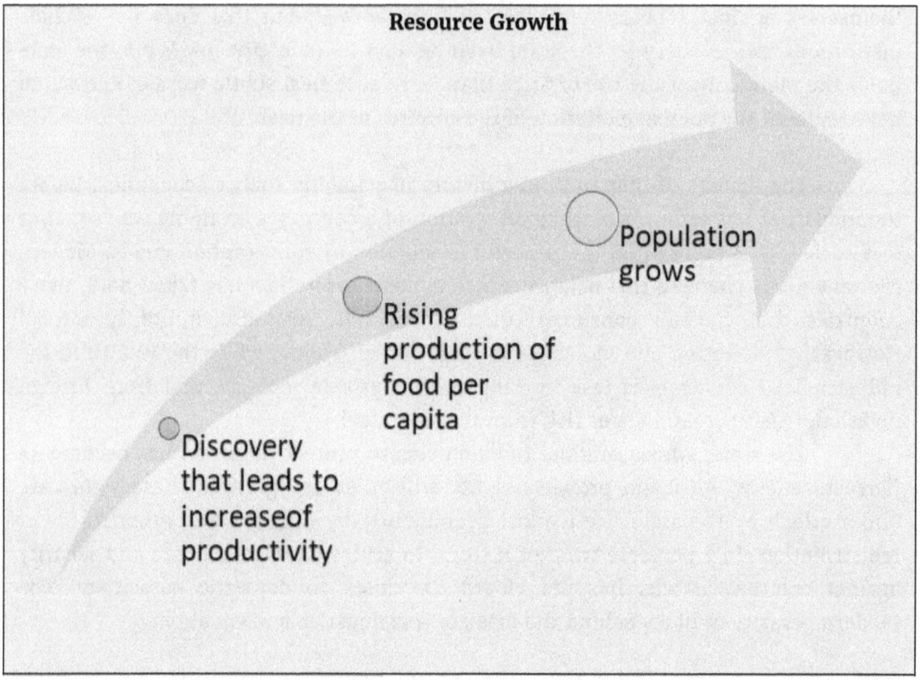

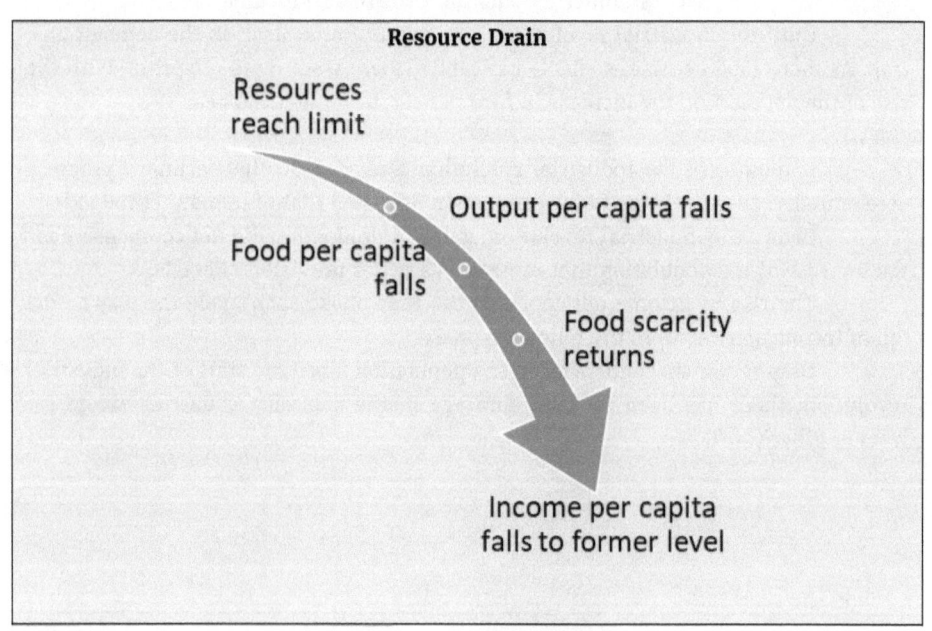

In the thousands of years before Christ, the world's population grew slowly. For the time around the birth of Christ, the estimates are between 150 and 300 million people in the world. Around 1850 the number of people on earth reached a billion for the first time.

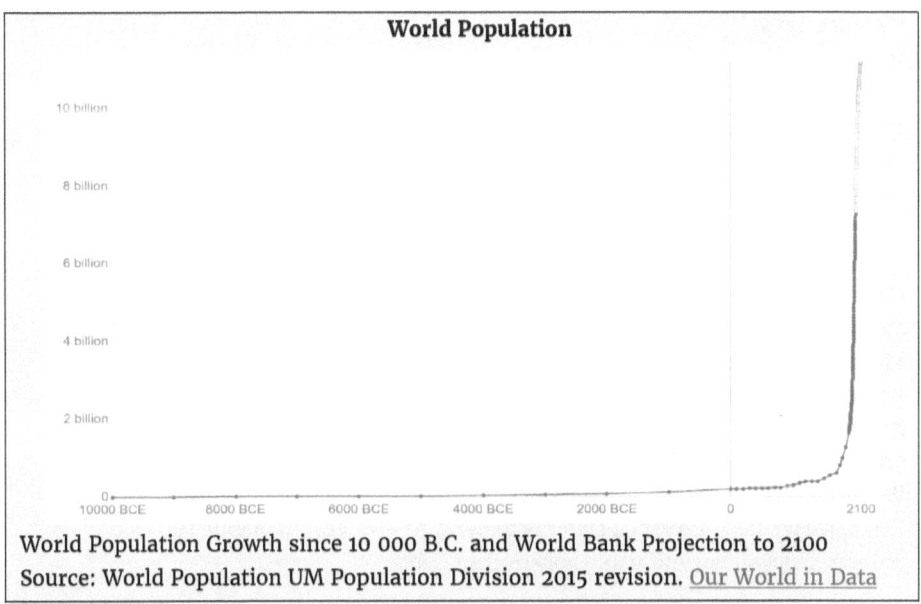

World Population Growth since 10 000 B.C. and World Bank Projection to 2100
Source: World Population UM Population Division 2015 revision. Our World in Data

In the meantime, the world's population has risen to seven billion.

Yet there is no reason to worry about a so-called 'overpopulation'. First, the growth rate of the population decreases after passing through the so-called 'demographic transition', and, second, there is enough space on earth. For a population density, such as exists in Paris, for example, the entire world population would occupy less space than is available in the State of Texas.

The population growth is about to stop because the reproduction rate is falling which is already the case.

From an annual growth rate of 2.1 % in the 1960s, the projections says that the annual growth rate of the world is to fall to a rate of 0.1 % in 2100.

In the early stages of development, the poverty, violence and population trap threaten economic progress. For the advanced economies, the hazards are the middle-income trap along with the imperialism and welfare trap.

***

Development Traps

Traps in the early stages of development

Poverty Trap

Insufficient savings inhibit capital accumulation, which in turn limits income and thereby savings

Violence Trap

In the short run, robbery is more effective than production, yet parasitic economies are not sustainable as they lead to the rise and fall of empires

Population Trap

While absolute production rises, per capita income stagnates as the rate of population growth exceeds the rate of the growth of production

Traps in the advanced stages of development

Middle Income Trap

Society opposes creative destruction and inhibits productivity advances. Politics strangles entrepreneurship through high taxes and bureaucracy

Imperialism Trap

In the short run, robbery is more effective than production, yet parasitic economies are not sustainable as they lead to the rise and fall of empires

Welfare Trap

Extensive welfare and social benefits undermine economic dynamic and lead to an economic slowdown and rising government debt

***

ECONOMICS OF WEALTH CREATION

Before the industrial revolution had brought about rising output per capita, higher incomes showed up only for short periods. Economic growth was too weak to compensate for the increase of the population that came with better nourishment. The increase of the population reverted the advantage of higher incomes. After a temporary rise, per capita income fell again. Over the millenniums before the capitalist economic take-off, the world population had grown but the per capita income had not risen. On average, the population before 1800 was not much richer than in the hundreds of hundreds of years before.

Before the industrial revolution, only the families in power achieved a high consumption level. Living standards depended on one's social rank in the hierarchy of exploitation, i.e. whether one belonged to the conquerors or to those who were the conquered. Throughout history, conquerors achieved higher living standards at the expense of the subjugated peoples. Yet the peace that conquerors have tried to establish after their settlement has remained precarious and all parasitic robbery economies have failed.

In order to achieve wealth through capital accumulation, peaceful conditions are necessary. The means to gain one's living must shift from the political to the economical method. Property rights must gain universal respect. They require protection - both domestically and against violence from the outside. Secure property rights is an essential requisite of capital accumulation. Accumulating capital consists of investments that will yield its income in the future while the consumption loss takes place in the present. If there is too much uncertainty as to the future returns, investment will not take place because then it would be more rational to consume than to save for later.

Backgrounder: Time Preference

Time-preference denotes how much an individual prefers immediate consumption over future consumption. The time preference trade-off requires reducing the present consumption level to get more consumption in the future. The lower the time preference the more the individual prefers higher future consumption and will give up present consumption to realize this preference. Economic growth requires diminishing time-preference and have less consumption now as the way to consume more later.

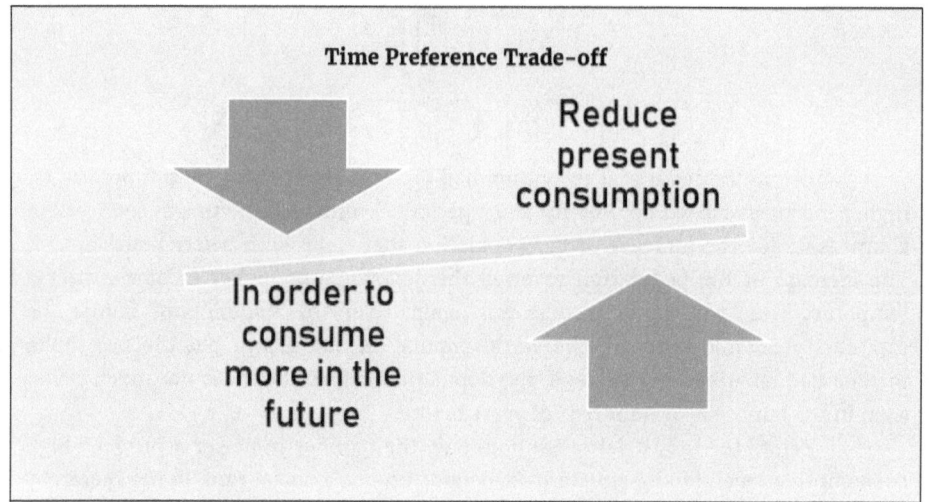

Human action in time confronts the choice between earlier or later. Time-preference is not a psychological concept but follows from the theory of human action. Time-preference is a praxeological principle. Without preference for earlier over later consumption, action could not take place but would turn itself into eternal waiting.

Human valuation takes place in the presence although the time horizon of individual valuation may go beyond one's lifetime and even towards eternity. The orientation towards the future results from the principle of human action, and preference-ranking pertaining to the future is its necessary condition. Any human action involves sequence and thus implies a ranking process that extends into the future.

There is no such thing as the so-called 'paradox of savings'. What is important for an economy to grow is a low time preference. Time preference is the tendency of human action to estimate the value of current and near consumption higher than the future consumption.

Time preference is necessary to survive from day to day. Yet in as much as economic growth requires investment and therefore savings, a lower time preference is necessary to gain a higher future consumption level. It is of little help to have a hundred-fold meal in a month if there is no food on the table for the next few weeks. Time preference is therefore reasonable. On the other hand, capital accumulation results in a higher income only later, which makes a lower time preference necessary.

Less consumption now is the way to have a higher consumption later. The meaning of savings is not austerity but to have more. The time preference rises when gaining profits is risky, and when uncertainty rises. In the face of the risks of confiscation, savings and investment come to a standstill because time preference will rise. This has been the case most of the time throughout history. As a consequence, economic growth and thus the income per capita has been stagnating.

***

It was not until around 1800 that the industrial revolution broke the vicious cycle of poverty, violence, and demography. Based on the knowledge from the preceding centuries and its diffusion through books and magazines as well as because of the rise of education, humankind could free itself from the shackles of the traps that had inhibited wealth creation before.

As incomes in the industry rose and women could free themselves from family dependency on their own merit - first as a factory girl and later as a professional - the birth rate fell while productivity progressed. In the course of this development, the wealth per capita of the population in Western societies has risen manifold over the past two hundred years.

Capitalist profit recycling

After overcoming the population trap and taming violence, protecting property gained importance, a process which led to the modern legal systems. Western industrialized countries established a system of law, which institutionalized private property of the means of production.

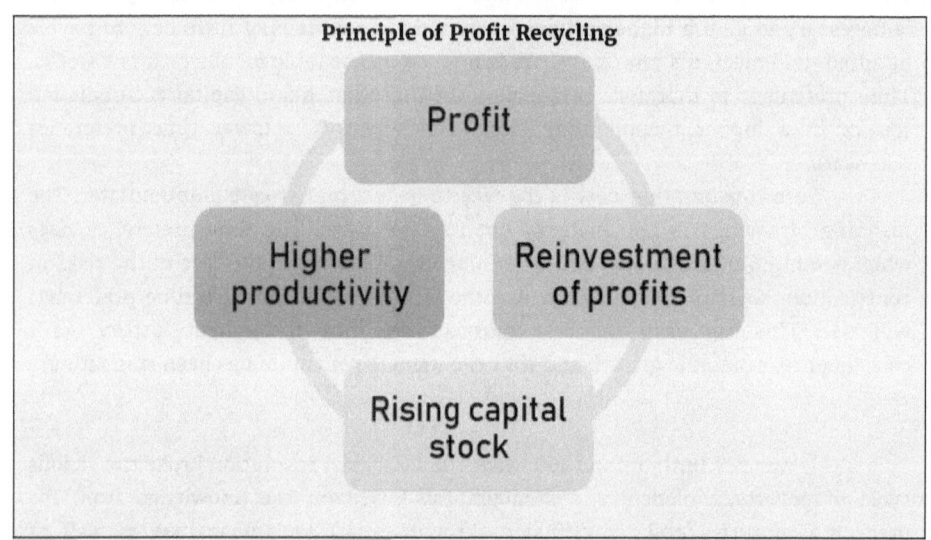

The decoupling of economic progress from population growth took place when the pace of technological progress surpassed the rate of reproduction. The key for this to happen was when companies emerged as profit-seeking entities that invested large parts of their current profits back into new enterprises to earn more profits.

The socialist ideology does not oppose property rights but wants to change them from a private right into a public domain. The socialists argue that with protecting the property rights of the means of production, the modern economy produces a class society the same way as it had been before in history. They lament exploitation under capitalism as if there were a strict division between those who suffer from the exploitation and those who exploit. Yet modern capitalism differs from the class societies of the past and from the caste societies. First, under capitalism, the social ranks do no longer come through birth; second, the workforce of the modern economy does not exist only in capitalists and proletarians but there are many intermediate forms; third, in the capitalist market economy, social positions change because innovation makes existing privileges obsolete.

In the world of political ideas, the liberalism of the 19th century put forth the right of private ownership of the goods of production. The violence that had been the essence of the state found a new task is to protect property. In the past, the state derived a precarious legitimacy from its function of serving as a political means of getting the livelihood of a ruling class. The classical liberal state, in contrast, received its legitimacy as the guarantor of the property rights in the interests of the whole population. Protection of property by state power is the core of the economic and social doctrine of classical liberalism. Consequently, protecting individual property was the point at which socialism directed its assault.

Classical liberalism is based on individualism and 'right' is not an issue of groups but of individual persons.

An individual has a natural right to property, including the property of the means of production (capital). For classical liberalism, justice does not pertain to the equality of results but what matters is the equality of opportunity. Classical liberalism does not negate the role of the state. However, it wants to limit its scope.

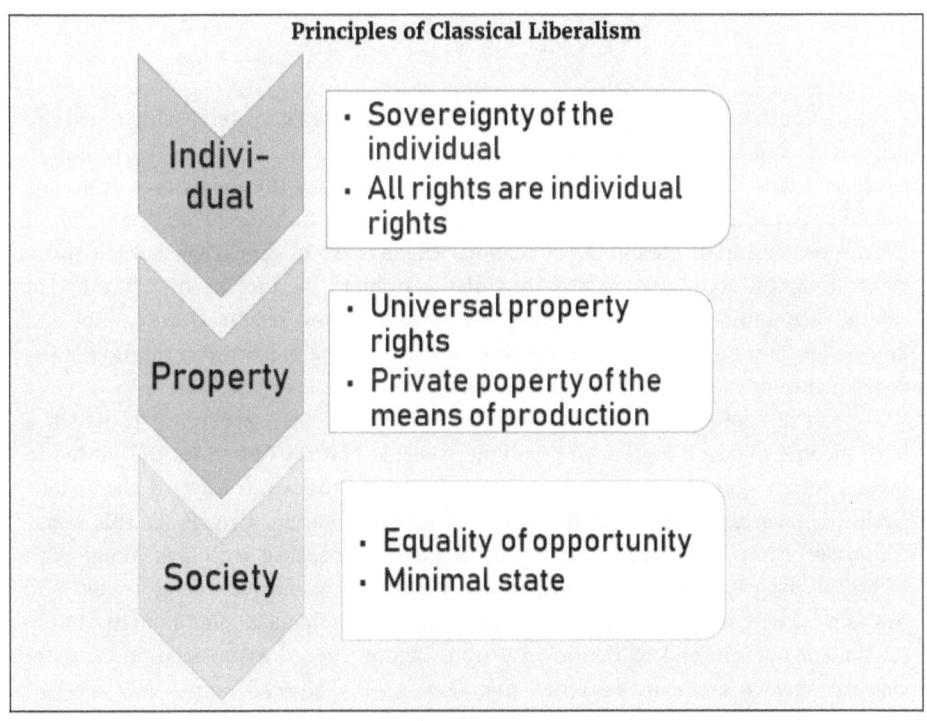

Antony P. Mueller

CAPITAL AND KNOWLEDGE

Capitalism triumphed because it is that economic system, which leads to prosperity and because with wealth comes power. Capitalism spread by imitation because it was more successful as a source of supremacy than the other economic systems. A capitalist economy means market competition based on the right of private ownership of means of production. The essence of capitalism is the private right of capital accumulation and thus of the right to the income from the use of capital. Economic growth as a rising per capita income results from capital and knowledge as it began with the industrial revolution. The industrial revolution is the consequence of the triumph of capitalism over other forms of production.

The capitalist economies entered the wealth cycle, according to which a high income makes a high saving volume possible and thus provides the means to invest, which again leads to more wealth. This way, the world escaped the vicious circle of poverty and entered the circle of wealth creation. Growth in this sense comprises capital accumulation, which is possible because it comes along with technical progress. The resulting higher productivity enables rising wages and incomes, which, in turn, lead to more capital: physical, financial, and human capital. Capitalism puts an end to the poverty trap. Before the industrial revolution, there was the vicious circle in existence that low-income allowed only a low level of savings and therefore there had always been a scarcity of productive investment.

Productivity

Productivity relates output (production) to input. According to the type input-factor, one distinguishes between total factor productivity, labor productivity, capital productivity and national productivity.

Types of Productivity

Total factor productivity	Labor (hour) productivity	Capital productivity	National productivity
• Total output/Total input	• Output per unit of labor • Output per hour worked	• Output per unit of capital	• Output (gross domestic product) per capita • National income per capita

Total factor productivity relates total output to total input. As such, input includes all factors of production such as labor, capital, and technology.

Labor productivity is limited to non-farm output and labor. Labor productivity is an important determinant of wages.

Capital productivity measures output per unit of capital.

The indicator 'gross domestic product per capita' represents output in terms of the gross domestic product divided by the number of the residents in a country.

***

Capitalism is an economic system, in which capital accumulation comes along with expanding knowledge in the form of technical progress. Because of innovations, capitalist growth is not quantitative, but qualitative. Capitalist economic growth results from the supply of better, cheaper and more diverse products, which originate from a production process whose focus is cost-efficiency and innovation.

Technological progress is crucial since the mere accumulation of capital finds its limit in diminishing marginal returns of capital. Each additional unity of capital produces lower marginal returns when technical knowledge and population remain constant. At the same time, the costs to preserve capital continue to rise. Without technical progress, the economy would come to a halt when the costs to uphold the capital are higher than the yield of capital. Then the capital stock must shrink.

No economy can maintain a production process where the depreciation rate exceeds the necessary amount of investment for its maintenance. For an economy to grow in terms of income per capita there must be technical progress. The richer a national economy and consequently the higher the capital stock already is, the more important is technical progress. The more mature an economy, the more important become human capital and technology.

For some period, economic growth can take place based on savings and capital accumulation. More investment leads to a higher capital stock and to a higher income. This process, however, works only until the economy confronts the fundamental dilemma that the rates of return on capital fall behind the marginal costs of maintaining the capital stock. Capitalism means a permanent change, and this applies to the capital structure. Without technical progress, the economy falls into stagnation.

If capital accumulation happens because of the incentives that come from expansive economic policies, the marginal costs of capital maintenance surpass the returns of the additional capital accumulation. Such policies must fail because the stimulus leads to a constellation where the income from capital is lower than the costs of capital preservation. Therefore, investment is not always beneficial. An expansive economic policy results in the opposite of the intention when the measures stimulate the accumulation of more capital than savings can support. The driving force of economic growth must not be government but private business on an unhampered market.

Human capital means having productive skills. A higher level of human capital leads to more returns of the existing stock of physical capital. An increase in human capital results in higher incomes with no increasing the share of physical capital because human capital allows a better use of the available capital goods.

Beyond the physical and human capital, income will rise when commerce intensifies because it allows a more intense division of labor. Domestically and internationally, free trade allows the economic actors to specialize in those activities where they enjoy a comparative advantage. Under free trade, all participants will enjoy a higher income because of this productivity effect. Increasing commercialization at the local, regional, national and global level means that the economic performance improves and that incomes rise.

Fundamentals of wealth creation

Economic growth occurs as roundabout production. Instead of producing a product directly, the production of an intermediate good takes place.

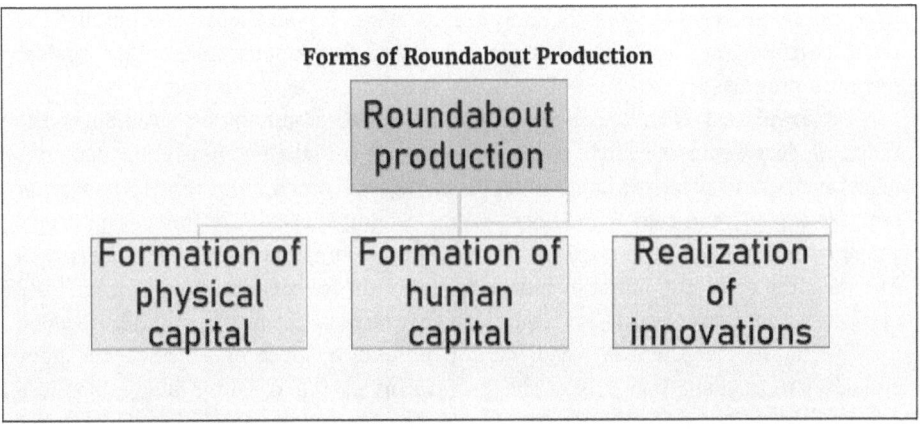

The intermediate production good, once finished, then serves to increase the productivity. The capital stock represents the totality of the production goods in its role as means to produce other goods.

Human capital includes the quality of human work, which comes from training and gaining skills.

Innovation is the application of new ideas to the production process. Innovation includes new products, new production methods, the opening of new markets and implementing new organizational forms. Ideas lead to new products, better and products, and to a greater variety and quality of goods.

***

Innovation is the entrepreneurial realization of business ideas. The function of the entrepreneur is to put ideas into practice to increase productivity and to earn higher profits. Business ideas express human creativity. They are an intellectual phenomenon. Economic progress happens when resolute entrepreneurs put these creative thoughts into practice. Economic growth depends on the ability of industry to generate innovation. Yet economic growth requires also a society, which tolerates and favors technological progress. Throughout history, technical progress has met with resistance. Technological knowledge is a recipe or a manual about how one can increase the productive effects of human labor in its interplay with capital and nature. Economic growth results from ideas put into profitable market operations. Only a few new ideas qualify as an innovation. Whether a business idea becomes an innovation depends on the market – whether the product finds buyers. In a market economy, the profitability determines the quality of an innovation.

One cannot realize innovations smoothly and without disruption. By its nature, innovation is disruptive and as such, it encounters resistance. The opposition to economic progress includes not only technical and financial obstacles but also the social barriers, the resistance that some parts of the population mobilize against technical progress.

Combined with technical progress, capital accumulation overcomes the limits of decreasing marginal return of capital. Yet realizing innovation demands investments, and therefore there must be savings to launch innovations. Innovation requires capital, and capital requires savings. Savings necessitate foregoing current consumption in favor of investment to gain a higher consumption level in the future. The meaning of saving is not austerity but more future consumption. Saving is the opposite of austerity. Saving is a technique that refrains from using up all the wood for heating so that there is wood left for building a house or a bridge and have enough left to plant new trees. The purpose of saving is better living, not less consumption. The same holds for human capital. Instead of using all available labor time in the present, a part of it goes into training to have better abilities and skills. Besides savings, innovation requires experimentation. The innovators try out new ideas or production forms instead of using the same process of production or always producing the same products. Therefore, economic growth needs liberty.

ECONOMIC FREEDOM

Innovation is the basis of economic growth. Innovation requires freedom in all its forms. Therefore, liberty is the foundation of economic growth and thus of prosperity. Innovation needs the liberty of private initiative and the freedom of information. Mere ideas are not enough. Innovation requires communication. Sharing ideas needs means of making new ideas public. This is, on the one hand, a technical problem and touches on the question of the means of the available communication techniques. On the other hand, the spread of economic progress requires open markets and entrepreneurial freedom. Both thrive where there is a high general level of freedom of expression.

Political and commercial freedom go hand in hand. Innovation must become public to find a market. Whether an innovation is successful or not depends to a large degree on how fast it turns into profitable sales. Product promotion is important for new products. In this respect, the invention of book printing with movable letters was a crucial precursor to the industrial revolution, since it made the production of books and the distribution of ideas inexpensive and more effective than before. Only modern electronic communication, particularly the Internet, has a comparable effect.

Innovation is creative destruction, and as such, it encounters resistance. The more economic and political might are interconnected, the easier it is for the owners of the economic power to block innovations with political means. This was the case in many places in the past. America was the first great exception.

The economic triumph of the United States rests, among other things, on the fact that there have been fewer obstacles to the spread of ideas in the United States than in most other countries. As early as in the eighteenth century, because of freedom of religion, there was freedom of expression and freedom of publication, while in most other parts of the world political censorship prevailed. Early in the history of United States, its newspaper industry began to flourish. America was also a leader in literacy and in general education. After all, the US was the country, which, with its independence, also introduced freedom of trade among its States, thus laying the foundations for American entrepreneurship. The more a country or region prescribes itself to the free market economy, the more it promotes economic advancement. The protectionist policy of the United States in the 19th century was not aimed against free trade as such. The US trade policy served to divert trade from Europe to trade among the States of the Union where a new area of free trade was being created.

In the USA, freedom of religion, freedom of expression, and freedom of the press existed together with the freedom of entrepreneurial activity, which owned little or nothing to political power. If one did not like the East Coast or did not fit, Americans would move to the West and escape the established powers with every mile they went further away. After the end of the American War of Secession (1861-1865), an extended period of economic growth began, which led to a long series of consumption-oriented innovations, especially at the turn of the century. While on the old continent, the breakthroughs of inventions happened mainly with investment goods, there were significant innovations going on in the consumer goods market in the US towards the end of the 19th century. In a short time, the reality of mass consumption should come into existence and change the economy, first in the United States and then, step by step, in the rest of the world.

Life today differs from that of our ancestors because innovations such as telephone, refrigerator, radio, movies, TV, automobiles, and restaurant chains have changed everyday life.

Economic growth has brought things into the hands of ordinary people, about which even the mightiest rulers of the past could only dream of and not even that because they did not understand that such things as any ordinary consumer nowadays can buy, could even exist. Today, the average wage earner in the developed industrialized countries is much better off than the richest and most powerful persons were before the industrial revolution. Even poor families possess most of the modern standard goods. The reason for this success is the freedom of expression and of the free entrepreneurial activity based on private initiative and the market economy. Nevertheless, both fundaments are always in danger, also in America.

Yet even the United States is not immune from a relapse into censorship. This was so during the War of Independence, the War of Secession, and during the First and Second World Wars. Today, a new form of censorship is taking shape, as freedom of expression is restricted under the tyranny of political correctness and the influence of special interests. In addition, there is a growing power in the hands of a jurisprudence that operates against business and innovation. It is not surprising that with suppressing the freedom of expression came the time of the decline of economic freedom. In the USA, towards the end of the second decade of the new millennium, entrepreneurial activity is in danger. In the international ranking of economic freedom, the US is moving downwards in the ranks while censorship ravages university campuses in the form of political correctness.

United States. Economic Freedom

The United States faces the risk of falling into the trap of the downward spiral where economic weakness leads to policies that reinforce the decline. The more the United States falls back in growth in the future, the more other countries will have the courage to step forth and to establish full freedom of expression and freedom of the press and of entrepreneurial activity.

The United States suffers from the growth of government. Size and scope of the state are expanding, and the regulatory and tax burdens are rising. Among the broad population the feeling gains momentum that the game is rigged. The perception is growing that America suffers from cronyism, elite privilege, and corruption. America's competitiveness is declining. Domestic and foreign debt is on the rise.

The US economic freedom index of the Heritage Foundation has fallen from 81 points and number in 2006 to an overall score of 75.1 and a world rank of 17 in 2017.

Economic growth is the source of prosperity. The opposition to economic growth means to be against affluence and to favor misery. Growth requires as its basis a solid ownership structure of private property, entrepreneurial freedom, and a competitive market order. This is the basic idea of Laissez-faire. To be against Laissez-faire means to be against economic growth and implies to be in favor of keeping people poor instead of making the world more prosperous.

The institutions that will replace the traditional state after its abolishment must confine itself to protect property rights. The more reliable such a protective institution will accomplish its task the more business can concentrate on production. The present state does neither protect property nor life. On the contrary, the modern administrative state is the most severe violator of property rights – more than private criminals. State intervention begins with the imposition of taxation and ends with the draft. First, the state demands your property, then your life. This way, the state, which supposedly represents the organ of protection of property rights, sabotages economic activity. Instead of fostering entrepreneurship and commitment to work, the state regulates and taxes capital and work up to the hilt.

The modern administrative state imposes taxes on labor like it does on tobacco and on alcohol as if work were venom, which government must tax to restrict its commerce. Taxes and contributions make labor more expensive and reduce its use. The absurdity of the modern tax state shows up in the fact that it burdens the activities with taxes on which the existence of the fiscal state itself depends. The income tax is a child of the 20th century. It is the indispensable complement of the war-and-welfare state, as it began to unfold already before the world plunged into World War I. The personal income tax is the most anti-liberal taxation and the worst of all taxes.

The labor force suffers not only from the burden of taxes and contributions. The state also intervenes in the wage-setting - whether by means of minimum wages or by the many other labor market regulations. Before someone can work, i.e. perform the all-natural human activity, one must obtain a permit. In many countries of the world, the legal process to open a business is a bureaucratic hurdle that is lengthy, expensive and unpredictable. It is no wonder that those countries are poor where it is the most difficult to set up a company and that countries with a high per capita income have a low threshold to entrepreneurship. The consequence of this interference is subdued economic growth.

Political power is an enemy of economic growth. This has been the case throughout history. Nowadays likewise, the powerful groups in society try to exclude new competitors. They do this with the help of the state by means of difficult bureaucratic regulations, complicated tax laws, and high barriers to market entry. The larger and the older a company the easier is it for such a firm to cope with the regulations. Bureaucracy and taxes are a serious obstacle for new companies that want to enter a market. Regulations push up the costs and establish barriers to entry. Opaque and contradictory bureaucratic legislation means that fewer companies will surmount these barriers to challenge established companies. Those few new companies that enter markets often could only do that not because of the quality of their product but because of their legal savvy and political connections.

Laws against the dismissal of redundant labor force make it difficult to reduce the costs when a project should fail. Job protection means that the existing work-places become more secure at the cost of job creation that would come with new projects. To avoid risks, the creation of new jobs falls, particularly for positions that come with a new project when there is no flexible labor market and the company must bear the risk to remain stuck with an overload of workers who cannot be fired. The more innovative, the more daring a project the more it must face the risk of failure. As such, start-up companies as innovators must consider fiasco and prepare for it. The more regulation and tax burden business face the more companies will refrain from new ventures. The government wants to 'save jobs', but what it does is to reduce the number of jobs available, particularly jobs that would be more productive.

Technological progress means increased productivity and thus a higher wage level. Trade unions are unable to raise the general average wage when productivity stagnates. Trade union power can only redistribute income among the workers themselves. Therefore, a strike aims in the first instance against the other workers in the other industries, which do not or do not yet go on strike. Whatever the idealistic intentions may be, union power hinders economic growth, prevents creating new and better jobs, and stifles economic growth. Yet because prosperity depends on economic growth, the workers themselves bear the costs of strikes and excessive wage claims. Apparent protection comes with the loss of the chance of higher prosperity. Under socialism, the state manages the economy. The jobs, wages, and prices are stable the same way as they are for the inmates of a prison. The protection that the administrative state provides comes with the stagnation of income and mass poverty of the working population. Prosperity needs economic growth, and economic growth needs entrepreneurial freedom.

Economic freedom and social progress

There is a strong link between economic freedom and income, and between economic freedom and social progress.

The freer the economy of a country, the more pronounced social mobility and the more favorable are other measures of social progress such as health, environment, human development, participation, and reduction of poverty. The causal chain runs from economic freedom to economic growth and higher income, and thus to social progress.

Indices of Economic freedom and of social progress

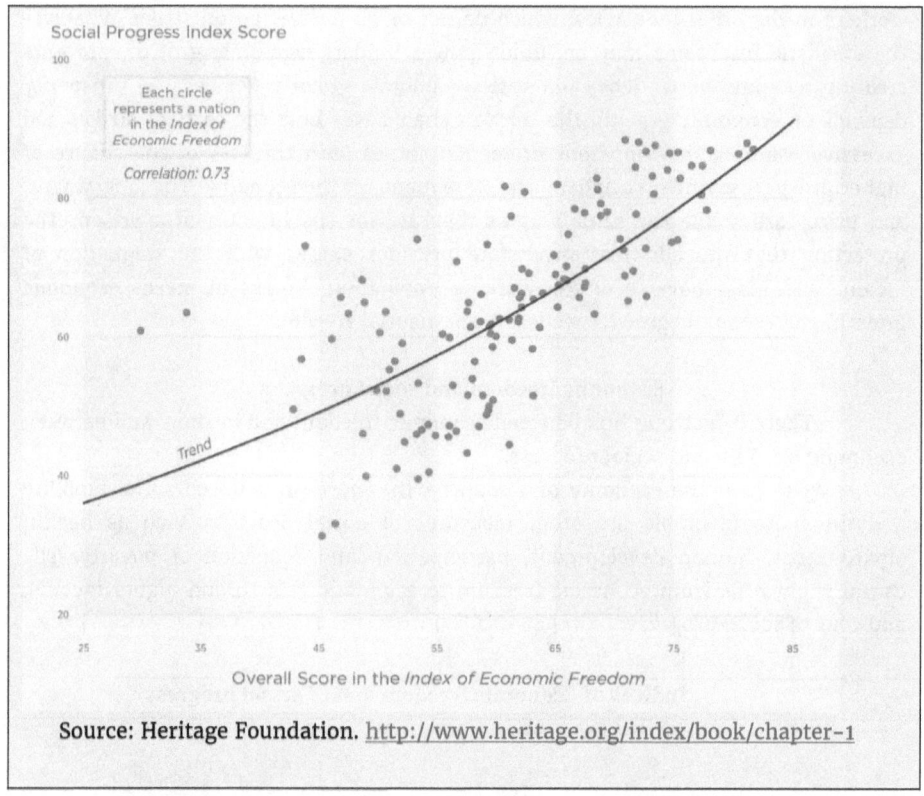

Source: Heritage Foundation. http://www.heritage.org/index/book/chapter-1

Economic growth is not just about getting bigger, but about a better adaption of the production structure to the wants and needs of the consumers. All inventions serve to satisfy existing basic needs - food, clothing, housing, transport, communication, entertainment, etc. – in a cheaper and better way. Investing involves dispensing with current consumption in some cases to achieve a higher consumption level in the future.

Economic growth requires material and human capital and presupposes the reduction of temporary consumption. Saving provides the funding of investments and forms the basis of economic growth when capital accumulation comes along with innovation. However, no saving takes place in the economy at the aggregate when the savings of a person A serves for the consumption of another person B as it is the case when people buy government bonds. If someone invests in bonds, it looks as though this person is saving, but, in fact, while this person abstains from consumption he provides the funds to the state that spends it to finance the consumption of other groups of persons and provide funds for wasteful public projects. Money that comes from the sale of bonds serves to pay pensions and other consumptive expenditures by the state. When a government incurs a budget deficit, the state is de facto dis-saving and by the amount of the deficit, overall macroeconomic savings fall.

Time preference is a necessity for human survival. Time preference urges human action to eat, to sleep, and not to postpone consumption forever to tomorrow and beyond.

However, economic growth requires temporary abstention from consumption, which means that the time preference must be subject to voluntary control. In general, countries with a population that have a low time preference, where a culture of disciplined waiting prevails, have a higher tendency to save and invest. A lower time preference results in a higher rate of accumulation of capital and leads to a higher growth rate compared to populations with a higher time preference. The cultural foundation of economic growth exists in the degree to which some people control their time preference.

There is a similar dilemma regarding the time preference as is the poverty trap. The poorer the people are the more urgent is the satisfaction of the immediate desires. This urge involves high time preference. In contrast, pre-existing wealth facilitates the temporary renunciation of desires in the expectation that a higher level of prosperity will come later by this postponement of present wishes.

A low time preference promotes saving and thus investment and capital formation as the basis for economic growth and thus the increase in wealth. As time goes by, the time preference decreases as capital accumulation progresses.

Backgrounder:
Interest, Consumption, and Savings

The nominal market interest rate results from the interaction between the money supply and the current and expected price level.

The time preference determines the natural real interest rate as the discount rate between current and future goods and thus the relationship between consumption and saving.

Determinants of the interest rate

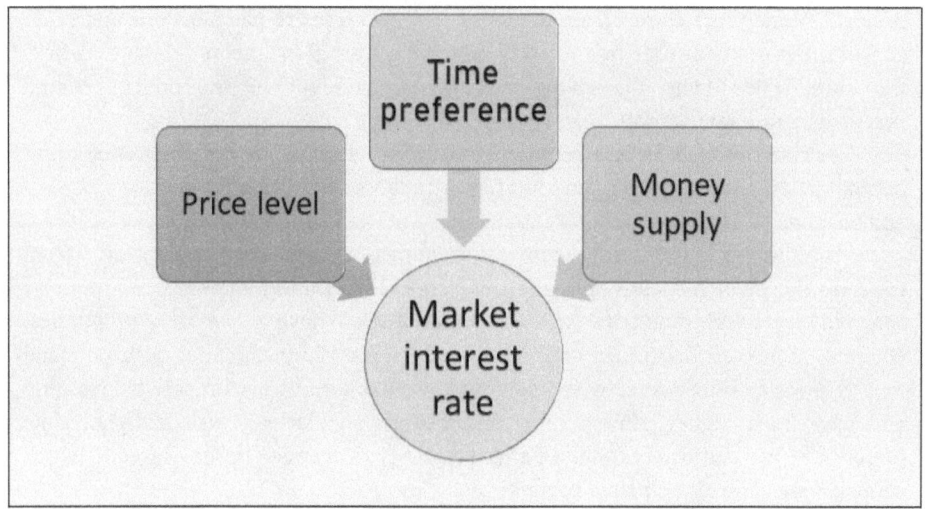

A high time preference means that present goods are highly valued compared to future goods of the same type. Accordingly, the natural interest rate increases. The more uncertain the future, the more the time preferences increases and the higher is the natural interest rate. If one were to know for certain, for example, that the world would go under tomorrow, the time preference would become infinite and correspondingly would the natural interest rate. Conversely, eternal life would imply a zero-rate time preference and a zero-interest rate. The degree of time preference depends on expectations.

The natural interest rate is the relative distribution of consumption and saving. The higher the time preference and thus the natural interest rate, the more people prefer consumption over savings.

Consumption, Savings, and Time Preference

> **Consumption**
> rising time preference
>
> **Savings**
> falling time preference

Insofar as the savings volume determines the level of investment, investments depend on the time preference. This explains why a falling market rate does not necessarily lead to an increase in investment.

The central bank determines the policy interest rate based on the control of the monetary base. Inflationary expectations of the market participants determine the market rate.

However, the actual volume of consumption and savings, and thus the investment, depends on the time preference.

In extreme cases, the interest rate may fall to zero or even below zero, and still not stimulate investment when the time preference is high and therefore a high natural interest rate prevails.

> **Risk Perception and Savings**
>
>
> **Risk of confiscation of property and income lifts time preference**
>
>
> **Rising time preference leads to less savings and less investment**

***

In order to carry out productive roundabout ways of production, there must be reserves available, which ensure that the workers and their families receive provision during the process of producing the investment goods. Roundabout production implies that investment does not yet yield a return, which will come only at the end of the process and not during the investment phase. While routine capital accumulation is less uncertain than an innovation, it brings less marginal returns. Innovation, in contrast, while it results in higher margins, suffers from uncertainty about success or failure. Therefore, it is crucial that there are companies that generate profits and that reinvest these profits. Excessive corporate taxes quash technological progress. Different from routine production, new projects are uncertain, but if they succeed, they bring high returns. Economic progress depends on making such innovative investments.

Value creation and capital structure

The production process extends over numerous stages, but the proceeds show up only at the end of the process when the goods arrive at the consumer and the latter pays for them. So long as the consumer does not pay for the final product, capitalists must pre-finance all the previous stages of production. The capitalist production process takes place as roundabout production. Instead of procuring one's livelihood directly with the mere force of pure labor, an intermediate material is produced as an investment good which facilitates the production of the desired consumer goods. Roundabout production increases the productivity of human labor.

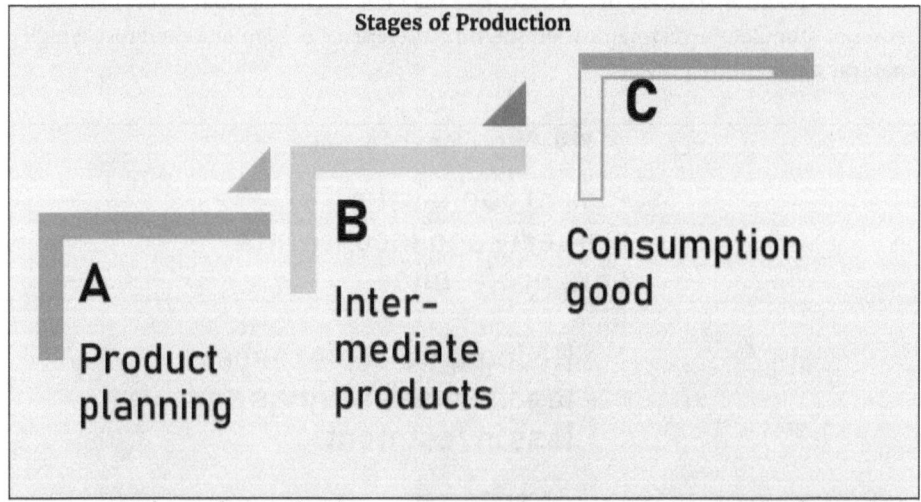

To have the production process running, one must maintain the capital structure. Yet the salaried workers demand their payment before the products are ready for consumption. The function of the capitalists lies in providing the funds that are necessary to maintain the capital structure. The contribution of the capitalists to the production is to maintain and expand the capital structure and to advance the salaries and wages before the consumers buy the product.

The extent of roundabout production depends on the size of the means of subsistence. Therefore, one cannot take the highest degree of productivity as the guideline, but to which extent resources are available for the period during which the intermediate product is on its way to final consumption. During roundabout production, the labor force that is employed in the roundabout process does not immediately produce goods that serve for consumption. Those who are active in roundabout production must receive their subsistence out of a present fund of available consumption goods. It is only later, when the consumers pay for the goods, that the capitalists receive their compensation. Capitalists have been waiting for the completion of the roundabout production process and have assumed the risks whether production will come to a successful end, and they only get their reward at the end of the process when the consumer pays.

Antony P. Mueller

THE STATE AS AN ENEMY OF GROWTH

In a free market economy, there is a natural tendency to expand production and to innovate. Stagnation afflicts the market economy through wrong economic policies. While the poverty trap hampers the way out of poverty, and the violence trap and the population trap block the road to wealth, the 'middle-income trap' hits the emerging economies when they oppose creative destruction. When a country has surpassed the traps of poverty, violence, and population, the path to prosperity is not open if the society does not yet embrace creative destruction. If at this stage of development, a country prefers social security to innovation, it will remain stuck in the middle-income trap. This is the case with many developing countries. The dominant class in these countries does not tolerate the changes that come with innovation and which challenge established positions of wealth. Consequently, economic progress slows down and comes to a standstill. The security that comes with social policy appears at first as a rise of prosperity – as more 'welfare' and more 'social justice' - when in fact it is the first step to economic stagnation. In the end, average incomes will fall as much as welfare policies diminish or block innovation and thereby lower the economy's productivity rate.

People opt for welfare and a 'social state' because they believe that it comes at no costs and provides only benefits. If people knew how the social benefits now imply less income later, the population, in general, would have a critical attitude towards the welfare state and politicians would have a harder time selling their fraud. Just as it is with security over liberty, a society that attributes a higher value to social security than to prosperity loses both. Promoting short-termism as it is inherent to a democracy run by political parties promotes the distribution of the cake and neglects that the goods must be produced before they can be distributed, and that the production should also grow over time. The illusion is widespread and propagated by the political machinery that production is independent of its distribution so that one could redistribute without weakening production.

Most of the 'distributive justice' is practiced at the expense of the 'commutative justice'. The justice of the distribution has its other side in the justice pertaining to the production of things. One cannot limit the idea of justice to distribution without contradictions. The rules of righteousness for the values of a society must include principles that reward personal achievement. The disregard of the commutative aspect of justice is itself unjust. It is also irrational since distribution is possible only when there is something to distribute, i.e. that production takes place after at all. Redistribution is unjust and economically irrational because it punishes those who carry on production and its advancement. When redistributing income and wealth becomes excessive, the active part of the population withdraws from production and parasitism takes over. This way, society will impoverish, and the poor are left with nothing. In the end, the poor themselves will pay the price because they will be the hardest hit when growth falters and unemployment rise.

It is problematic to strife towards more justice. Justice is often a false concern. The reality of life proves that coincidences in the form of happiness and misfortune undermine intentional righteousness. Justice and equality are not of this world. The costs to impose equality exceed its benefits because we are all children of luck – good and bad. It is important to stop the welfare state in time because its negative effect on economic growth is not visible. For some time, capital consumption compensates for weak economic growth. When this happens, it does not yet show in the national statistics. Statistically, consumption counts as a contribution to national production. An increase in consumption, even if it comes at the cost of capital formation and is due to the consumption of capital, gets counted as economic growth, although it is a statistical illusion.

An insidious form of capital consumption takes place through government debt. A deficit of the government budget means that the national savings volume falls and that the economic investment potential has become smaller. In the economic statistics, the expenditures – whether they are from the state or from the private side – are equally a contribution to the social product. Yet while the spending benefits the current receivers of the government expenditures, the lower capital formation will later show up in a weaker economic growth. In as much as public debt is an enemy of economic growth, it is also an enemy of wealth creation. The benefits that a government distributes in the short run financed by higher public debt will reduce further economic growth and make poverty persistent in the long run.

A new phase of weak economic growth has arisen in the industrialized countries because of the expanding national debt, which began in the 1970s and has continued until our present days. The industrialized nations must now learn how difficult it is to get out of the whirlpool. This is most noticeable in the decline in the rate of productivity progress experienced by large industrialized countries since the

1970s, along with the strong expansion of the welfare state and the rise in public debt.

Government debt diminishes the economic growth dynamics. Weak economic growth, in turn, leads to higher government expenditures and thus a rising debt burden. When an economy experiences faltering growth, the demand for social benefits increases even more. This redistribution leads again to less growth. Numerous countries have fallen into the trap where social expenditures weaken the economy and where this weakness requires more spending, which in turn weakens the economy. A dangerous side effect of this fall into a downward moving spiral is that the anti-capitalistic attitude in the population increases, since for most citizens, the causal links are difficult to ascertain.

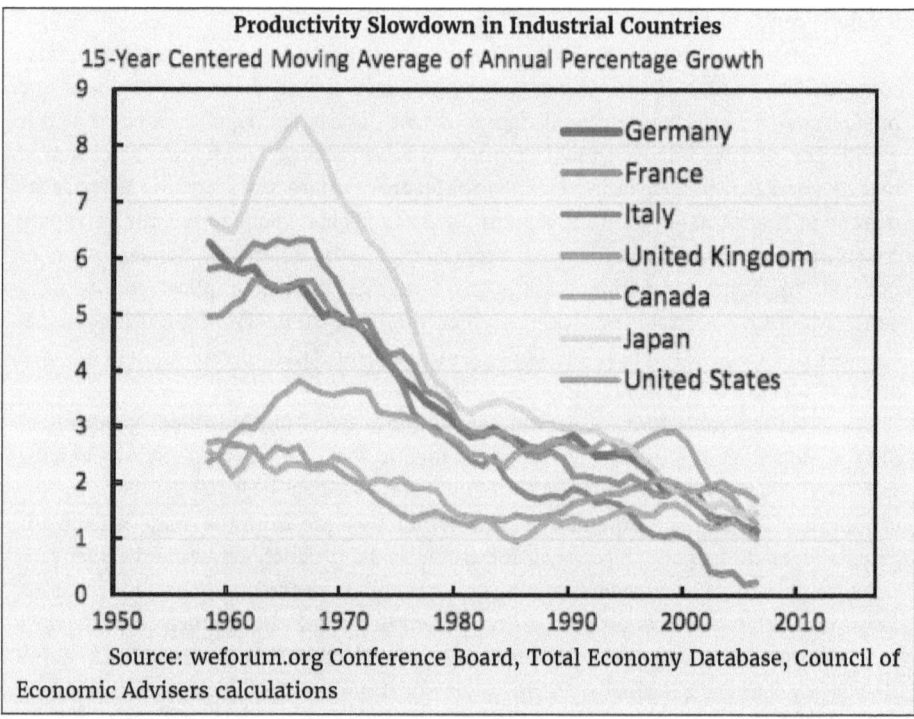

Source: weforum.org Conference Board, Total Economy Database, Council of Economic Advisers calculations

The welfare state and public debt are the main causes of the decline in the productivity rates. The productivity of a country determines the income level.

Over the past decades, the rates of the annual increase of productivity of the major industrialized countries have fallen from an average of five percent in the late to around two percent in the 1990s and keep on falling.

Without productivity gains, there is no increase in real per capita income.

The expansion of the welfare state leads to a rising public debt, which weakens the economic performance. A weakening economy entails more welfare spending and leads to a further rise of public debt, which, in turn, leads to more welfare spending.

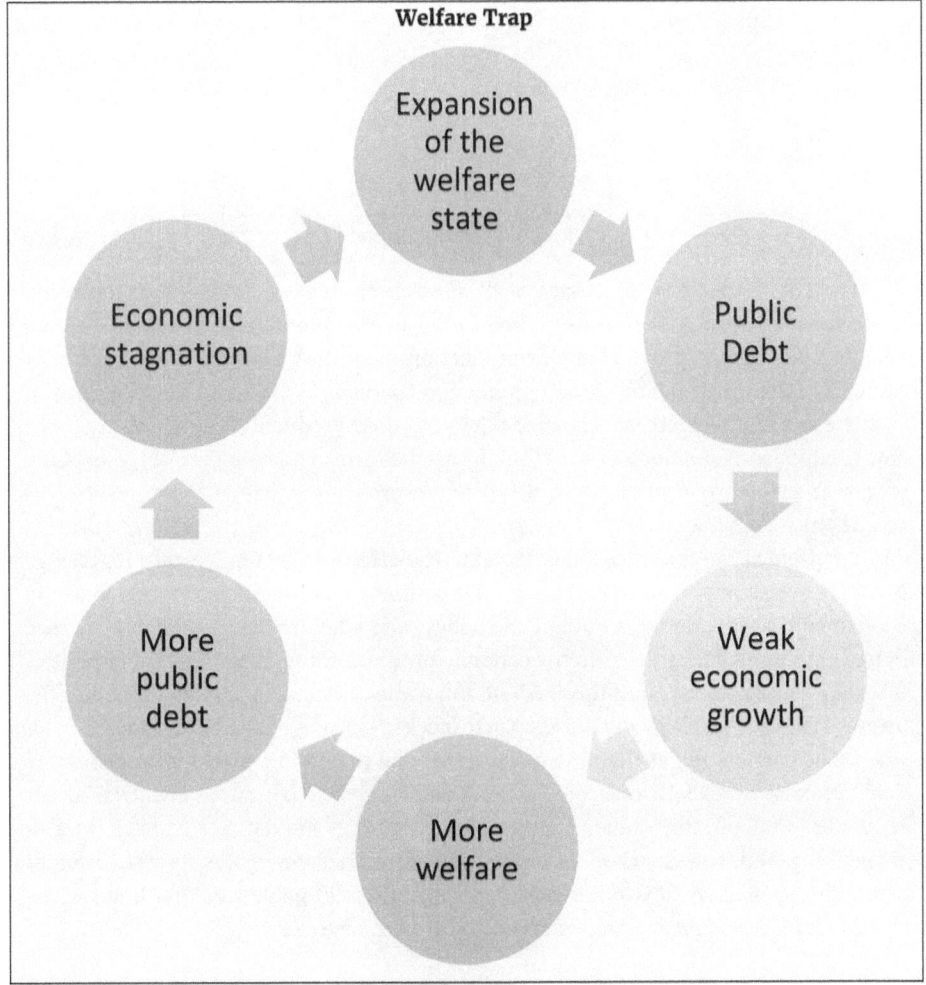

CREATIVE DESTRUCTION

The progress that comes with innovation makes other goods obsolete. Modernization means that some other forms of the production of goods become outdated. Less competitive forms of production must disappear from the market or the companies must change their production methods. With the disappearance of obsolete goods, the sources of income related to their production do also vanish. Any new production technology or new organizational form renders a part of the existing economic structure useless. Any new, better product makes the old goods less attractive.

Innovation is creative destruction. The effects of technological progress go beyond the economy and affect society and politics. If the social resistance is strong enough so that it can take a hold of the policy, and when social movements succeed in blocking innovation, the gate to economic progress shuts down. The more politics takes up the resistance from those whom innovation affects negatively, the more the future economic growth will falter. Such blockades have existed for thousands of years. The barriers fell at the time of the industrial revolution. There is no guarantee that the dark times will not come back. The same way that some countries never adopted capitalism, the modern industrialized countries are not free from the risk of abandoning the free market economy. The fact that the gates to the road of prosperity opened about two hundred years ago does not guarantee that innovations will go on forever. The enemies of economic growth never rest.

Obstacles to innovation

It is not only the bureaucracy, which hinders innovation but also traditions and institutions. Tradition will result in social resistance and abort innovation because of superstition. The modern superstitions come in a scientific clad. There are also institutions that hamper innovation and its propagation along with underdeveloped financial markets and closed markets.

The best promotion of innovation is not through subsidies but to reduce the obstacles to innovation, such as bureaucratic regulations and high taxes.

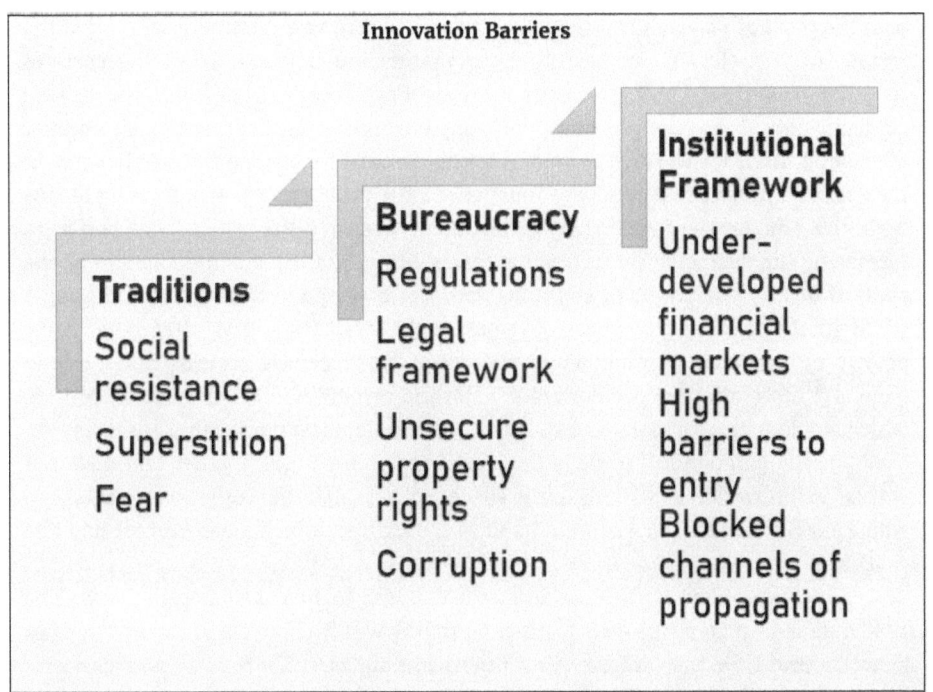

***

The opponents to innovation find their allies not only in politics but also with some business leaders who are afraid of losing their pre-eminence when innovations threaten their realms. While the effect of protection is visible to those who receive its benefits, the indirect loss of prosperity remains undetected and therefore has no representation in the political play. When the spirit of innovation and economic progress declines, the economy grows less, falls into stagnation, and shrinks. Then, even more, the call for action by the state rises, albeit the policy itself has caused the problem. The voters want higher income and redistribution in their favor, and the government follows the call - just to make things worse.

Nowadays, governments are doing both: on the one hand, they suppress and slow down the structural change caused by the innovation; on the other hand, especially in the military sector, they promote 'research'. While it is obvious that the state that suppresses innovation hinders economic growth, it is less clear that this is also the case when the state promotes innovation and research for the state's particular aims.

While in the case of private research projects, business companies must bear the costs of research from the outset and will receive a remuneration only if the result of the project is successful on the market, public funds cover the costs of research. For state funding - both for university research and with the private company subsidies - the grants flow already during the development phase and not at the end. In other words, the state does not reward innovation but participates in the cost of a project that promises innovation. The problem of public funding begins with the standards of selection. Government agencies are in no way better in foreseeing the technological future than private business. To obtain public funds, the applications for the grants of subsidies need not correspond to the aim of earning a profit in the market-place but must please the evaluators. Too often, the whole project of 'research funding' ends with only the expenses covered and nothing gained. A more effective promotion of innovation would be low tax rates on profits, which would incite companies to innovate and develop new marketable products.

The competition itself is the discovery process. The market test does not consist in innovation as such or in the so-called 'research' but rather to the extent to which the innovation can maintain itself in the market, which means that it must be profitable.

The problem with innovations is not just to invent something new. The challenge is to market the new product so that it will find buyers and that the sales generate profit for the company. Inventions are not rare. There is an abundance of useless inventions and there is no lack of fascinating business ideas without a proper market. There is no reason for the state to promote more ideas. What is lacking in using inventions is capital, and capital is in short supply because too little is saved. Due to capital shortages, there are usually much more potential technological projects available that could be profitably realized.

There is an overhang of productivity-enhancing possibilities that find no use when savings are too low. If the economy is not yet rich enough to afford the new technology, inventions remain unused. Just as a low-income person can only afford a bicycle but not a motorcycle although the motorcycle is much faster, an economy cannot have the most productive standard of capital in all its sectors. The limit of economic growth does not come from an absence of technological ideas but from a lack of capital to realize the ideas.

Public debt is an enemy of economic growth. Because budget deficits reduce overall savings, investment suffers and economic growth falters. If the government promotes innovation and accumulates debt, it will hamper economic growth in two ways: first, by lowering the efficiency of the economy, and, second, by crowding-out private research through the less productive public research funding.

The implementation of profitable innovations characterizes the entrepreneur as depicted by Joseph Alois Schumpeter (1883-1950) in his work on the economic development of 1911. The entrepreneur is not necessarily an inventor or a manager but someone who directs production and markets ideas with the aim of turning them into a profitable enterprise on the market. Entrepreneurs are rare. If their income moves to dizzying heights, this is because of their exceptional performance. Most of the entrepreneurial performance remains obscured to the observers. One sees the success that shines in the daylight, forgets the failed attempts, and disregards those entrepreneurs who have remained unsuccessful, and therefore have disappeared.

If the free market is functioning, competition eradicates the weaker businesses so that the system approaches an optimum without ever reaching it. In competitive markets, profits must be high enough to compensate for the high risk of failure. When a successful company emerges and gains prominence, it faces competition from imitation of the product and its improvement. Competitive innovation erodes the profit of the pioneer. Monopoly gains resulting from innovation are not permanent. Economic progress makes products obsolete. This is why profits must be high for the pioneer to maintain the incentive to innovate.

The basis for growth is industrial clusters, which do not owe their existence to an organization but appear as spontaneous orders, which do not obey hierarchical commands but thrive following their own laws of development. The rules of a spontaneous order are not explicit. A spontaneous order has neither a syllabus nor an organizational map. To know the rules of such a spontaneous order, one must participate in the game. One cannot learn the tricks of the trade outside of the circus. To be successful, one must be an insider and participate in the activity of the spontaneous order itself. One cannot transplant and simply imitate a spontaneous order. Innovation requires being a player. This is the way to become familiar with the details that are necessary for the success of the innovation. The problem with the state is not only that it is not a team player but that the state is as much a collaborator as an opponent with divergent interests and mutually exclusive projects.

In development policy, the lack of insight that simple imitation in the form of a state-run 'industrial policy' will fail has cost a high price to the poor countries that adopted such policies. With the industrial policy in the developed countries, it is not much different. The planning of new industries by the state is an unsolvable task and a sign of hubris because the technological future is unforeseeable. New technologies and industries themselves must discover the paths to success because there is no way that could be known before some venture proves that it works. The way of economic progress is experimental and cannot be planned. Innovations emerge, they are not implanted. Innovations thrive in the environment of a spontaneous order, not in organizations.

Return Matrix of Venture Capital Projects

	Consensus	No consensus
Failure	negative	negative
Success	neutral	positive

Failure means a negative result whether there was a consensus or not. The project earns no profit. Normal profits emerge when the project is successful but came into being based on consensus. Many other investors also spotted the opportunity and invested in the project as well. The result is neutral. No exceptional profits come about. Only a project that is successful and was launched without consensus reaps positive results and earns extraordinary profits.

The need to propose projects that meet consensus condemns the public financing of innovation projects to notorious underperformers. Promotion for research and development with the assistance of government usually takes place for ordinary projects, which, even when they are successful, will earn only meager profits.

Projects that earn a high return are naturally those that do not find a consensus at their beginning.

ECONOMIC KNOWLEDGE

One can imagine the competitive exploration process as a procedure where the pioneer companies explore the unknown terrain and develop the new markets while the rest imitates and improves the innovation. Pioneer profits serve as an incentive to take the risk of innovation.

The freer an economy is, the more the companies can embark upon an economic discovery process and create new products and new measures of production. In due course, the profit of the pioneer company melts away and the gains pass on to the consumers in the form of more goods and cheaper and improved products.

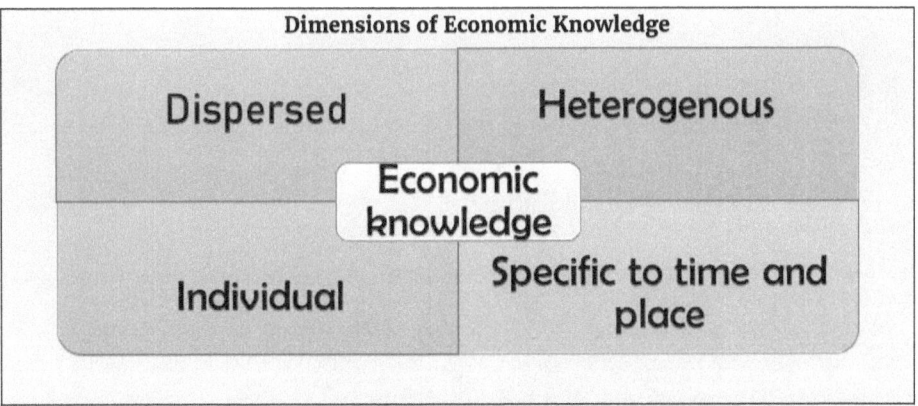

Innovation requires individual companies, which explore like scouts the path to the future. Nobody knows from the outset, which new products will find acceptance in the market, and how and where the technological breakthroughs will happen. Following the terminology of Friedrich Hayek, competition is a procedure of discovery.

Competition is a procedure to generate economic knowledge. The competitive process reveals knowledge that is specific to time and place. As such it exists in the mind of the individual. Economic knowledge is neither homogenous nor concentrated but dispersed and heterogeneous. It is the essence of the competitive process that the knowledge of the actors differs from individual to individual and changes with the situational setting.

The innovation, which first manifests itself in the success of the pioneer enterprise, reaches the consumers as a higher standard of living. Imitation follows and spreads the innovation in various new forms throughout the economy. Imitation is more difficult than it seems. One must be part of the competition process to imitate in a smart way. Innovation does not come out of nowhere but forms part of the market process. Therefore, the catch-up process of the developing countries is so cumbersome.

Developing countries suffer from the lack of deep markets. Even when there should be generous financing available to launch an individual investment projects, development does not spread across the economy because a product never stands alone in the market but forms part of a larger grouping of goods and industries that operate as clusters and whose ramifications reach across regions, nations, and continents. The barrier to development is not the lack of funds but the lack of a competitive market system where many firms try to gain profits and reinvest these profits to launch new and better goods.

FREE TRADE

International trade expands the size of the market. The individual firms have more potential customers and the companies can become more specialized and more productive. Higher productivity increases wages. The economies involved in international trade get richer, while the isolated, self-sufficient economies remain poor.

In order to participate in international trade, it is not necessary that a company is more productive in all its branches than its competitors abroad. Trade does not depend on the absolute level of productivity but on the comparative cost advantages. This means that also those companies and their employees benefit from free trade, whose competitiveness is lower than other companies. There is no reason to withdraw from international competition because one is less productive if the productive unit has a comparative cost advantage. Comparative advantage means to give up those areas of production where one is very much at a disadvantage and concentrate on those economic activities where one is less disadvantaged. Even in the case that companies in one country are less competitive than those abroad, foreign trade would be beneficial. External trade allows abandoning the activities of the lowest relative productivity in favor of those areas where the disadvantage is less. International competition has the same effect as to how competition works on the domestic markets. For the high-productivity country, international trade opens the possibility that its companies concentrate on the areas where they are not only more productive than the companies in other countries abut to focus on those areas of production where the companies are much more productive. In small markets, specialization is limited and thus production must include activities where productivity is low.

With the expansion of markets, the structure of the economy changes. The production in those areas where there are the greatest competitive disadvantages falls, while those where productivity is relatively strong, increases. If the trading partner has a higher level of productivity, the firms concentrate on the activities where they have the comparatively highest productivity. In the countries that participate in free trade, the general level of productivity increases because there is a shift of production to those companies that are relatively more productive. The less efficient enterprises focus on activities where the distance in productivity to the companies with the higher performance is lower. In terms of higher productivity, international trade benefits all participants. In each of the countries that begin to trade with one another, a re-allocation takes place according to the comparative advantages.

Wealth creation through free trade

The effect of global trade on wealth comes through specialization, which lifts productivity.

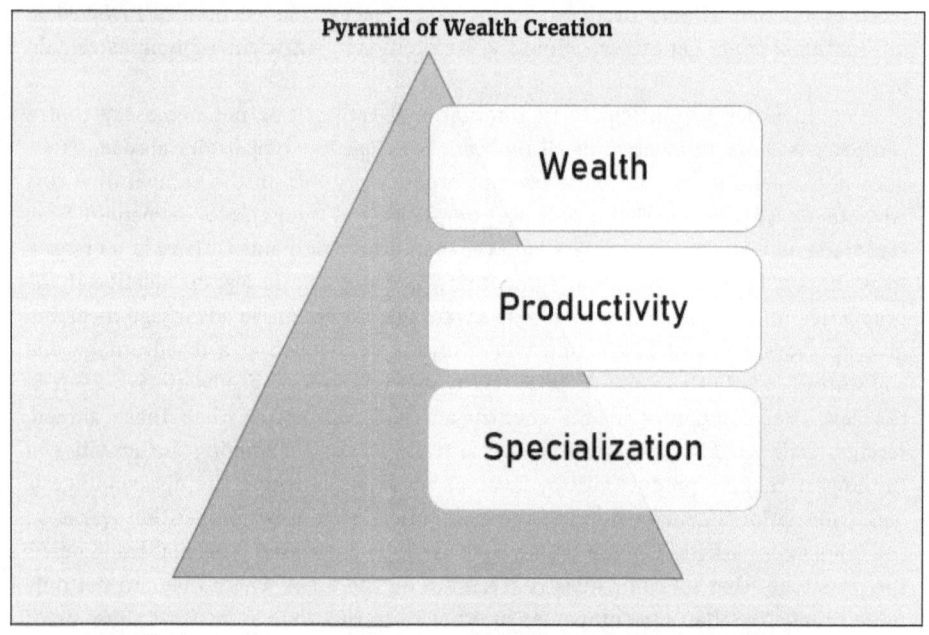

International trade means larger markets, and larger markets augment the scope of specialization. Rather than focusing on countries as the entities that specialize, it is individual companies that count. The larger the market becomes because of global trade the more individual companies can specialize and raise their productivity. Companies that produce goods that enjoy economies scale experience additional scale effects that comes with a larger market.

***

The competitive process compels the participating companies to move into areas where the opportunity costs are the lowest and to abandon the activities where they are high. International trade induces the firms to concentrate in those fields of production where their relative productivity is the highest. As each company produces those goods where its productivity is higher, the overall level of productivity increases. The wage level depends on productivity. By increasing the productivity, globalization increases the general level of world incomes. International competition boosts productivity and leads to more prosperity. Free trade makes the world rich - protectionism makes the world poor.

Higher productivity means that one achieves more output with the same amount of input of labor and capital. This way, the productivity increase leads to rising profits. Higher profits encourage the expansion of production. The more intense competition and the more companies take part the faster productivity gains spread throughout the economy and the faster productivity benefits consumers in the form of lower prices, better quality and a greater variety of products.

With most economic phenomena, people recognize only what is at the surface and see what happens in the short term. When discussing free trade, people favor protectionism because they think this is the way to help 'our industry' and to save 'our jobs'. Protectionists focus on that aspect of free trade that leads to extraordinary profits for some companies while in some other production areas, jobs get lost and even entire industries fail. While some companies prosper, other firms must close their doors. Some industries disappear in one country and emerge in another as they change location according to relative productivity. Yet what the protectionists fail to see is that it is the structural change, which brings about overall productivity and the rising wages. Resistance to free trade is equal to the opposition against other forms of economic change as it comes, for example, from technological progress.

The more a country involves itself in the world trade, the more the companies of this country must concentrate their activities on the niches where they can achieve a relatively higher performance. The higher productivity emerges together with a rising purchasing power of the inhabitants of this country. World trade enlarges the markets and intensifies the competition; the power of national enterprises diminishes as their relative market size falls. Free trade is a strong antidote to a monopolization of the economy.

Extension of the market size

International trade is the geographical extension of the national market, which, in turn, is the extension of the local market and of family exchange. The larger the extension of the market, the more the individual and the companies can specialize and thereby increase their productivity. Specialization implies the division of labor and capital, which, in turn, require markets. The integration of a country into the global market provides the full potential of specialization for this country's individuals and firms.

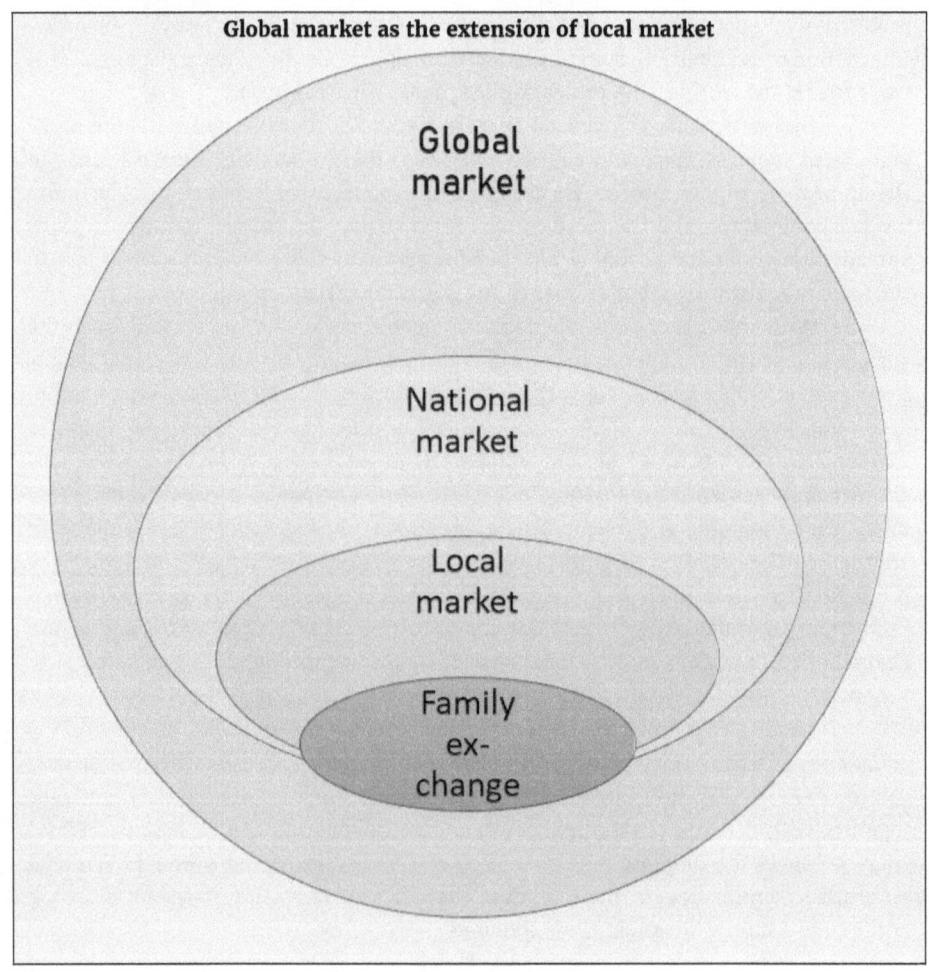

World trade extends the markets and lays the foundation for higher incomes as the expansion of the size of the economic area increases the potential for capital accumulation and innovation.

The larger the market, the more worthwhile becomes specialization and thus the acquisition of a specialized human capital.

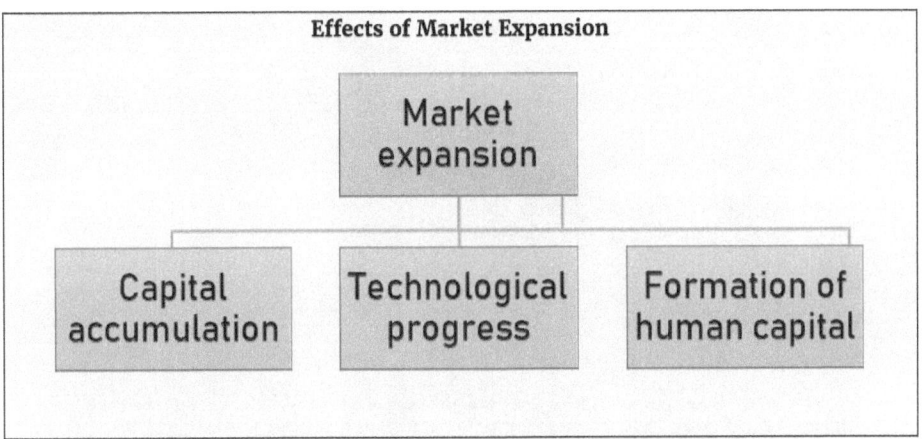

The result of world trade is a higher level of productivity. Productivity gains come also to the less productive economies as the respective firms in these economies will gain the opportunity to specialize in those areas where they are relatively better and when they abandon those activities where they are relatively more unproductive than their competitors abroad.

Not countries specialize in a system of free world trade, but enterprises. Companies apply specific capital and specialized human capital. With international competition, the level of knowledge and the specialization of capital of the companies is rising. This increases productivity and income.

***

Like commerce on the local and national level, world trade is an interplay of competition and cooperation. This process of association begins with the individual in the family and continues in the local and regional spheres to extend to the national economy and to international relations and to the global economy. The protectionists take the nation-state as their criterion for the limits of free trade. They do not recognize that if their arguments in favor of protectionism were correct, they should also apply regional and local criteria. If protectionism were so good for the nation, why not also impose tariffs for a specific region within a country?

Effects of free trade

When a country opens to free trade, it expands the market. With the extension of the markets come higher productivity and more product diversity. More competition and increased productivity lead to lower prices and a better product quality.

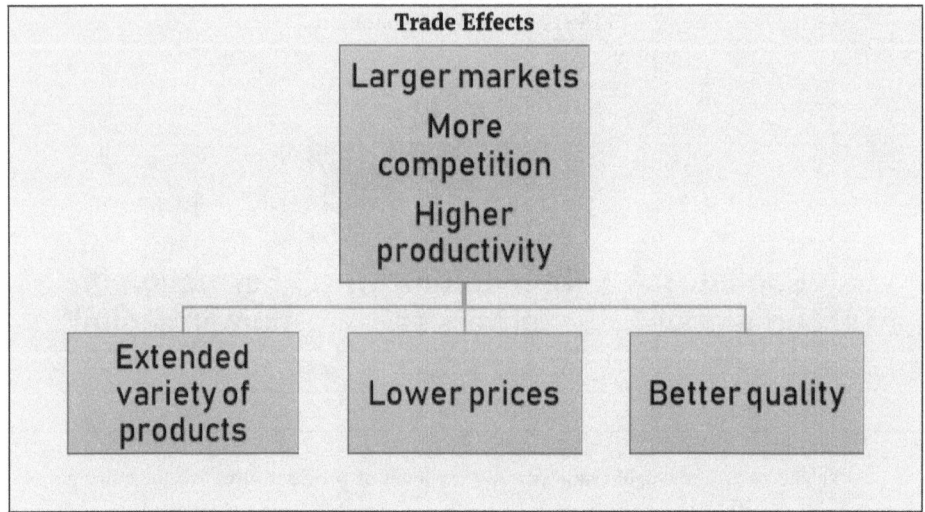

Free trade has effects like technical progress. The less productive firms make room for the more competitive companies. There is a shift of the factors of production to the sectors of higher productivity at the expense of the less productive sectors. This process lays the foundation for higher incomes. Free world trade serves the consumer through a wider product variety, lower prices, and better quality of the goods and services.

SUMMARY

Economic growth is not a self-purpose but serves to achieve a higher degree of satisfaction of the consumers. In this sense, economic progress does not exist mainly in more but in better products and in more diverse goods. The purpose of economic growth is to free people from poverty and to ease the pain of work. No system other than capitalism makes this possible because, in capitalism, growth takes place through innovation and productivity gains.

Technical progress makes it possible to achieve a higher yield with the same input of labor and capital. Economic growth, therefore, means that one can produce the desired goods in a shorter time and thus gain leisure time.

The beneficial effect of economic growth is the reward of saving time. People can transform the saved time into leisure or use it to develop and apply new ideas, which further increase the productivity of human labor and capital. Modern capitalism is an entrepreneurial capitalism because economic success comes from transforming ideas into goods and processes that pass the market test.

One of the main errors of economic policy is to focus on economic growth and employment instead of productivity gains. Yet what matters is productivity, and the best way to promote productivity is having a capitalist order of free markets.

The sources of wealth creation are commerce and innovation. Human creativity and the benefits of exchange are the keys to wealth. Those societies do well, which put the least resistance to these natural expressions of human action.

OUTLOOK

While the socialism of the Soviet pattern is not the dominant ideology of our time, the anti-capitalist mentality is still virulent, and this ideology is all over in the media, the schools, and the universities. The great error of the modern socialists, like that of their predecessors, is to believe that poverty originates from capitalism.

History has shown that socialism exists as a tyranny. With the choice of interventionism and socialism, economic stagnation comes, while the decision for a free market economy leads to economic progress. Theory and history confirm that socialism is inseparable from stagnation and oppression while capitalism is more productive the freer it is.

A look at the experiences with Communist rule makes the diagnosis unambiguous. Yet popular discontent runs against the capitalist economic order. There is a widespread illusion that one could have both the wealth of capitalism and the supposed socialist equality and justice.

The modern state has a structure that is very different from the original ideas of classical liberalism, and in some respects, it is the opposite. Instead of having less state, liberal democracy comes with more intervention; instead of more individual liberty, the current system has extended its control over the individual. The majority voting system in place leads to interventionism, and from there, socialism is only a step away. Democracy does not protect against folly or tyranny.

History does not have an inevitable path of development, but there are economic laws. The decision of this or that version of the economic system is free, but the consequences are not free to choose. Freedom refers to the choice of institutions, not to their consequences.

In this sense, there is a power of ideas, and at the same time, there is the impotence of ideas in the face of facts. There are situations where, as the saying goes, one cannot change things anymore. Before the wrong decision was made, the path was open as the options were laid on the table. A different choice could have evaded the problems that have surfaced now as a consequence of the wrong decision, and the course of history would have gone in another direction.

The alternatives are clear: on the one hand, free capitalism as an economic order that brings personal liberty and overall prosperity, and, on the other hand, the socialist command economy, leading to poverty and oppression. The 21st century will belong to those nations that choose the path to free capitalism.

FIGURES AND TABLES

WHAT IS CAPITALISM AND HOW DOES IT WORK?
- World Output and Real Gross Domestic Product (GDP) per capita
- Types of capital
- Capital as a factor of production
- Typology of capitalism
- Building blocks of modern capitalism
- Forbes List of billionaires 1987 and 2017
- US stock exchange since 1870
- Price-earnings ratios of American equities since 1870
- Macroeconomic constellations and investment strategy
- Driving forces of economic progress
- Exchange by barter and by money
- Pyramid of prosperity
- Personal well-being and income
- Extreme poverty since 1820
- China. GDP per capita
- Income per person relative to the United States 1960 vs 2008
- Distribution of the printing press in the 15th century
- Pillars of modern capitalism
- Factors that laid the groundwork of modern capitalism
- Preference ranking
- Determinants of value
- Chain of value determination and factor remuneration
- Information and incentive function of prices
- The market-process
- Interventionist spiral
- Price determination
- Competitive process
- Spread of consumer goods
- Life expectancy since 1800
- Distribution of world income 1820, 1970 and 2000
- Characteristics of modern capitalism
- Economic freedom and income

THE ECONOMICS AND POLITICS OF WEALTH CREATION
- Types of savings
- Poverty trap
- Parasitic economy
- Stages of parasitism
- Population trap
- World population growth since 10 000 BC
- World population growth and rate 1760-2100
- Development traps: Early Stages
- Development traps: Advanced Stages
- Time preference trade-off
- Capitalist profit recycling
- Principles of classical liberalism
- Productivity
- Forms of roundaboutness
- United States: Economic freedom index 2008-2017
- Economic freedom and social progress
- Determinants of interest rate
- Relation between consumption, savings, and time preference
- Risk perception and savings
- Stages of production
- Productivity slowdown in industrialized countries
- Welfare trap
- Innovation barriers
- Profit mix of venture capital projects
- Economic knowledge
- Wealth creation through free trade
- Global market as extension of local market
- Effects of market extension
- Effects of tree trade

BIBLIOGRAPHICAL REFERENCES

Achen, Christopher H. and Larry M. Bartels: Democracy for Realists: Why Elections Do Not Produce Responsive Government (Princeton Studies in Political Behavior) Princeton University Press 2017

Antonopoulos, Andreas M.: The Internet of Money. Merkle Bloom LLC. 2016

Applebaum, Anne: Gulag. A History. Anchor Books. 2004

Applebaum, Anne: Red Famine: Stalin's War on the Ukraine. Doubleday. 2017

Ashford, Nigel and Stephen Davis (eds.): A Dictionary of Conservative and Libertarian Thought (Routledge Revivals). Routledge. 2012

Bagus, Philipp: In Defense of Deflation (Financial and Monetary Policy Studies). Springer 2014

Bagus, Phillipp and Andreas Marquart: Blind Robbery!: How the Fed, Banks and Government Steal Our Money. FinanzBuch Verlag. 2016

Baldwin, Richard: The Great Convergence: Information Technology and the New Globalization. Belknap Press. 2016

Banerjee, Abhijit, and Esther Duflo: Poor Economics: A Radical Rethinking of the Way to Fight Global Poverty. Public Affairs. 2012

Barnett, Anthony: The Athenian Option: Radical Reform for the House of Lords (Sortition and Public Policy Book 5). Imprint Academic. 2017

Barrat, James: Our Final Invention: Artificial Intelligence and the End of the Human Era. St Martin's Griffin. 2015

Belke, Ansgar and Thorsten Polleit: Monetary Economics in Globalised Financial Markets. Springer. 2009

Belloc, Hilaire: The Servile State. T. N. Foulis 1912

Benda, Julien: The Treason of the Intellectuals. Routledge. 2006

Benson, Bruce L: The Enterprise of Law: Justice Without the State. Independent Institute. 2011

Birner, Jack and Pierre Garrouste (eds): Markets, Information and Communication: Austrian Perspectives on the Internet Economy (Routledge Foundations of the Market Economy). Routledge. 2003

Block, Walter: Defending the Undefendable. Ludwig von Mises Institute. 2008

Block, Walter: The Privatization of Roads and Highways: Human and Economic Factors. CreateSpace Independent Publishing Platform. 2012

Block, Walter: Toward a Libertarian Society. Ludwig von Mises Institute. 2014

Boaz, David (ed.). The Libertarian Reader: Classic & Contemporary Writings from Lao-Tzu to Milton Friedman. Simon & Schuster 2015

Boaz, David: The Libertarian Mind. A Manifesto for Freedom. Simon & Schuster. 2015

Boehm-Bawerk, Eugen von: Karl Marx and the Close of His System: A Criticism (Classic Reprint). Forgotten Books. 2012

Boehm-Bawerk, Eugen von: Positive Theory of Capital. Ludwig von Mises Institute. 2007

Bostroum, Nick: Superintelligence: Paths, Dangers, Strategies. Oxford University Press 2016

Boetie, Etienne de la: The Politics of Obedience: The Discourse of Voluntary Servitude. With an Introduction by Murray Rothbard. Ludwig von Mises Insitute. 2015

Boettke, Peter J.: Living Economics: Yesterday, Today, and Tomorrow (Independent Studies in Political Economy). Independent Institute. 2012

Boettke, Peter J.: Calculation and Coordination: Essays on Socialism and Transitional Political Economy (Routledge Foundations of the Market Economy). Routledge 2001

Boettke, Peter J.: The Oxford Handbook of Austrian Economics (Oxford Handbooks). Oxford University Press. 2015

Boettker, Peter J.: The Political Economy of Soviet Socialism: the Formative Years, 1918-1928. 1990th Edition. Springer 1990

Boldrin, Michele and David K. Levine. Against Intellectual Monopoly. Cambridge University Press. 2010

Bourdieu, Pierre: On the State: Lectures at the College de France, 1989 - 1992. Polity 2015

Bouricius, Terry: (S)election: Sortition, the democratic alternative (Fomite Interrogations: A Series of Tracts for Our Time) (Volume 6). Fomite Publishers 2017

Boyes, William J.: Managerial Economics: Markets and the Firm (Upper Level Economics Titles). South-Western College Publications. 2011

Brafman, Ori and Rod A. Becksstrom: The Starfish and the Spider: The Unstoppable Power of Leaderless Organizations. **Portfolio. 2008**

Brafman, Ori and Rod A. Becksstrom: The Starfish and the Spider: The Unstoppable Power of Leaderless Organizations. **Portfolio. 2008**

Brackins, Daniel Alexander: Private Property, the Law, and the State. CreateSpace Independent Publishing Platform. 2017

Braun, Eduard: Finance behind the Veil of Money. CreateSpace Independent Publishing Platform. 2016

Brennan, Jason: Against Democracy. Princeton University Press. 2016

Brick, Howard: Transcending Capitalism: Visions of a New Society in Modern American Thought. Cornell University Press. 2016

Brynjolfsson, Eric and Andrew McAfee: The Second Machine Age: Work, Progress, and Prosperity in a Time of Brilliant Technologies. W. W. Norton & Company. 2016
Buchanan, James and Richard Wagner: Democracy in Deficit. The Legacy of Lord Keynes. Emerald Group Publishing. 1977

Burnheim, John: The Demarchy Manifesto. For Better Public Policy **(Societas)**. Imprint Academic 2016

Burnheim, John: Is Democracy Possible? The Alternative to Electoral Politics. University of California Press. 1985

Burnheim, John: The Demarchy Manifesto: For Better Public Policy **(Societas)**. Imprint Academic. 2016

Bylund, Per L.: The Problem of Production: A new theory of the firm. Routledge 2015

Cachanosky, Nicolas: Monetary Equilibrium and Nominal Income Targeting (Routledge International Studies in Money and Banking). Routledge. 2018

Caplan, Bryan: The Case against Education: Why the Education System Is a Waste of Time and Money. Princeton University Press. 2018

Caplan, Bryan: The Myth of the Rational Voter: Why Democracies Choose Bad Policies. Princeton University Press. 2008

Chafuen, Alejandro A.: Faith and Liberty: The Economic Thought of the Late Scholastics (Studies in Ethics and Economics). Lexington Books. 2003

Christinsen, Clayton M.: The Innovator's Dilemma: When New Technologies Cause Great Firms to Fail (Management of Innovation and Change). Harvard Business Review Press. 2016

Clark, Gregory: A Farewell to Alms: A Brief Economic History of the World (The Princeton Economic History of the Western World). Princeton University Press. 2009

Cogan, John F.: The High Cost of Good Intentions: A History of U.S. Federal Entitlement Programs. Princeton University Press. 2017

Conquest, Robert: The Great Terror: A Reassessment 40th anniversary Edition. Oxford University Press. 2007

Conquest, Robert: The Harvest of Sorrow: Soviet Collectivization and the Terror-Famine. Oxford University Press; Reprint edition. 1987

Cowen, Tyler and Alex Tabarrok: Modern Principles of Economics. Worth Publishers. 2014

Cowen, Tyler: Average Is Over: Powering America Beyond the Age of the Great Stagnation. Plume. 2014

Cowen, Tyler: The Great Stagnation: How America Ate All the Low-Hanging Fruit of Modern History, Got Sick, and Will (Eventually) Feel Better. Dutton 2011

Coyne, Christopher J. and Abigail R. Hall: Tyranny Comes Home: The Domestic Fate of U.S. Militarism. Stanford University Press. 2018

Cwick, Paul F.: An Investigation of Inverted Yield Curves and Economic Downturns. Ludwig von Mises Institute.

Dahlen, Michael: Ending Big Government: The Essential Case for Capitalism and Freedom. Mill City Press. 2016

Dalrymple, Theodore: Nothing but Wickedness: The Origins of the Decline of Our Culture. Gibson Square Books. 2018

Davidson, James Dale and William Rees-Mogg: The Sovereign Individual: Mastering the Transition to the Information Age. Touchstone. 1999

Delannoi, Gil and Oliver Dowlen (eds.): Sortition: Theory and Practice (Sortition and Public Policy). Imprint Academic. 2010

Deneen, Patrick J.: Why Liberalism Failed (Politics and Culture). Yale University Press. 2018

Diamandis, Peter H. and Steven Kotler: Abundance: The Future Is Better Than You Think. Free Press. Reprint edition. 2014

Di Iorio, Francesco: Cognitive Autonomy and Methodological Individualism: The Interpretative Foundations of Social Life (Studies in Applied Philosophy, Epistemology and Rational Ethics). Springer 2015

Dilorenzo Thomas J.: How Capitalism Saved America: The Untold History of Our Country, from the Pilgrims to the Present. **Crown Forum. 2005**
Dilorenzo, Thomas: The Problem with Socialism. **Regnery Publishing. 2016**

Doherty, Brian: Radicals for Capitalism: A Freewheeling History of the Modern American Libertarian Movement. Public Affairs. 2008

Dorn, James A. (ed.): Monetary Alternatives: Rethinking Government Fiat Money. Cato Institute 2017

Dorn, James A., Steve H. Hanke and Alan A. Sir Walters (eds.); The Revolution in Development Economics. Cato Institute. 1998

Dowlen, Oliver: The Political Potential of Sortition: A study of the random selection of citizens for public office (Sortition and Public Policy). Imprint Academic 2009

Drochon, Hugo: Nietzsche's Great Politics. Princeton University Press. 2016
Drucker, Peter: Innovation and Entrepreneurship. HarperBusiness. 2006

Easterbrook, Gregg: It's Better Than It Looks: Reasons for Optimism in an Age of Fear. PublicAffairs. 2018

Easterly, William R.: The Elusive Quest for Growth: Economists' Adventures and Misadventures in the Tropics. **The MIT Press. 2002**

Easterly, William: The White Man's Burden: Why the West's Efforts to Aid the Rest Have Done So Much Ill and So Little Good. **Penguin. 2007**

Easterly, William R.: The Tyranny of Experts: Economists, Dictators, and the Forgotten Rights of the Poor. **Basic Books. 2015**

Ebeling, Richard and Jacob G. Hornberger: The Failure of America's Foreign Wars. Future of Freedom Foundation. 1996

Ebeling, Richard M.: Monetary Central Planning and the State. **The Future of Freedom Foundation. 2015**

Emerson, Ralph Waldo: The Essential Writings of Ralph Waldo Emerson (Modern Library Classics). Modern Library. 2000

Eire, N. N. Carlos: Reformations: The Early Modern World, 1450-1650. Yale University Press. 2016

Eucken, Walter: The Foundations of Economics: History and Theory in the Analysis of Economic Reality. Springer. 2011

Eusepi, Guiseppe and Richard E. Wagner: Public Debt: An Illusion of Democratic Political Economy (New Thinking in Political Economy series). Edward Elgar Publications. 2017

Erhard, Ludwig: Prosperity Through Competition. Praeger. 1958

Ertel, Wolfgang: Introduction to Artificial Intelligence (Undergraduate Topics in Computer Science). Springer 2018

Evans, Anthony J.: Markets for Managers: A Managerial Economics Primer (The Wiley Finance Series). Wiley. 2014

Evans, Michelle and Augusto Zimmermann(eds.): Global Perspectives on Subsidiarity (Ius Gentium: Comparative Perspectives on Law and Justice). Springer 2014

Evans, Stanton M.: Stalin's Secret Agents: The Subversion of Roosevelt's Government. Threshold Editions. 2013

Ebeling, Richard: Austrian Economics and Public Policy. Restoring Freedom and Prosperity. The Future of Freedom Foundation. 2016

Ferguson, Niall: The Square and the Tower: Networks and Power, from the Freemasons to Facebook. **Penguin Press. 2018**

Ferguson, Niall: Civilization: The West and the Rest. Penguin Books. 2012
Fareed, Zakaria: The Future of Freedom: Illiberal Democracy at Home and Abroad (Revised Edition). W. W. Norton & Company. 2007

Feyerabend, Paul: Against Method. Verso. 2010

Folsom, Burton W.: The Myth of the Robber Barons: A New Look at the Rise of Big Business in America. Young America Foundation. 1991

Ford, Martin: The Rise of the Robots: Technology and the Threat of a Jobless Future. Basic Book. Reprint edition. 2015

Foss, Nikolai J. and Peter Klein (eds.): Entrepreneurship and the Firm: Austrian Perspectives on Economic Organization. Edward Elgar Publishing. 2002

Frank, Malcolm, Paul Roehrig, Ben Pring: What To Do When Machines Do Everything: How to Get Ahead in a World of AI, Algorithms, Bots, and Big Data. Wiley 2017

Friedman, David D.: The Machinery of Freedom: Guide to Radical Capitalism. CreateSpace Independent Publishing Platform; 3rd edition. 2015

Friedman, Milton and Anna Jacobson Schwartz: A Monetary History of the United States, 1867-1960. Princeton University Press. 1971

Friedman, Milton: Capitalism and Freedom. Fortieth Anniversary Edition. University of Chicago Press. 2002

Fukuyama, Francis: The Origins of Political Order: From Prehuman Times to the French Revolution. Farrar, Straus and Giroux. 2012

Garrison, Roger: Time and Money: The Macroeconomics of Capital Structure (Routledge Foundations of the Market Economy) New Edition. Routledge 2007

Gatto, John Taylor: The Underground History of American Education, Volume I: An Intimate Investigation Into the Prison of Modern Schooling. Valor Academy 2017

Guerin, Daniel (ed.): No Gods No Masters: An Anthology of Anarchism. AK Press 2005

Giddens, Anthony: The Third Way: The Renewal of Social Democracy. Polity Press. 1999

Giddens, Anthony: Capitalism and Modern Social Theory: An Analysis of the Writings of Marx, Durkheim and Max Weber. Cambridge University Press. 1973

Goodwin, Barbara: Justice by Lottery (Sortition and Public Policy). Imprint Academic 2005

Gordon, Robert J. : The Rise and Fall of American Growth: The U.S. Standard of Living since the Civil War (The Princeton Economic History of the Western World). Princeton University Press 2017

Gordon, David: An Austro-Libertarian View: Current Affairs, Foreign Policy, American History, European History (Essays by David Gordon). 3 vols. The Ludwig von Mises Institute. 2017

Granovetter, Marc: Society and Economy: Framework and Principles. Belknap Press: An Imprint of Harvard University Press. 2017

Grant, James: The Forgotten Depression: 1921: The Crash That Cured Itself. Simon & Schuster. 2014

Halberstam, Davin: The Best and the Brightest. Modern Library. 2002

Harford, Tim: Fifty Inventions that Shaped the Modern Economy. Riverhead Books. 2017

Harris, Fred and Alan Curtis (eds.): Healing Our Divided Society: Investing in America Fifty Years after the Kerner Report. Temple University Press. 2018

Haskel, Jonathan and Stian Westlake: Capitalism without Capital: The Rise of the Intangible. Princeton University Press. 2017

Hathaway, Oona A. and Scott J. Shapiro: The Internationalists: How a Radical Plan to Outlaw War Remade the World. Simon & Schuster. 2017

Hayek, Friedrich A. von: Individualism and Economic Order. University of Chicago Press. 1996

Hayek, Friedrich A. von: The Constitution of Liberty: The Definitive Edition (The Collected Works of F. A. Hayek). University of Chicago Press. 2011

Hayek, Friedrich A. von: The Road to Serfdom: Text and Documents -The Definitive Edition (The Collected Works of F. A. Hayek, Volume 2). University of Chicago Press. 2007

Hayek, Friedrich A.: Denationalisation of Money. The Argument Refined. CreateSpace Independent Publishing Platform. 2014

Hazlitt, Henry: Economics in One Lesson: The Shortest and Surest Way to Understand Basic Economics. Crown Business. 1988

Hazlitt, Henry: The Failure of the New Economics. Martino Fine Books. 2016

Heidegger, Martin: The Question Concerning Technology, and Other Essays (Harper Perennial Modern Thought). Harper Perennial Modern Classics; Reissue edition. 2013

Hennig, Brett: The End of Politicians: Time for a Real Democracy. Unbound Digital. 2017

Herbener, Jeffrey M. : Pure Time-Preference Theory of Interest. Ludwig von Mises Institute. 2011

Heyne, Paul L., Peter J. Boettke, and David L. Prychito: The Economic Way of Thinking. Pearson Series in Economics. 2013

Hicks, Stephen, R. C.: Explaining Postmodernism: Skepticism and Socialism from Rousseau to Foucault (Expanded Edition). Ockham's Razor Publishers. 2011

Higgs, Robert: Against Leviathan: Government Power and a Free Society (Independent Studies in Political Economy). Independent Institute. 2004

Higgs, Robert: Crisis and Leviathan: Critical Episodes in the Growth of American Government, 25th Anniversary Edition (Independent Studies in Political Economy). Independent Institute; Anniversary edition. 2013

Higgs, Robert: Depression, War, and Cold War: Studies in Political Economy. Oxford University Press. 2006

Higgs, Robert: Taking a Stand: Reflections on Life, Liberty, and the Economy. Independent Institute. 2015

Hirschman, Albert O.: The Passions and the Interests. Political Arguments before its Triumph (Princeton Classics). Princeton University. 2013

Hirschmann, Albert O.: Exit, Voice, and Loyalty: Responses to Decline in Firms, Organizations, and States. Harvard University Press 1970

Holcombe, Randall G.: Advanced Introduction to Public Choice (Elgar Advanced Introductions series). Edward Elgar Publishers. 2016

Holcombe, Randall G.: Advanced Introduction to the Austrian School of Economics (Elgar Advanced Introductions series). Edgar Elgar Publishers. 2014

Holcombe, Randall G.: Producing Prosperity: An Inquiry into the Operation of the Market Process (Routledge Foundations of the Market Economy). Routledge 2015

Holcombe, Randall G.: Entrepreneurship and Economic Progress (Routledge Foundations of the Market Economy). Routledge 2006

Hoppe, Hans-Hermann: A Short History of Man: Progress and Decline. Ludwig von Mises Institute 2015

Hoppe, Hans-Hermann: A Theory of Socialism and Capitalism. Ludwig von Mises Institute. 2003

Hoppe, Hans-Hermann: Democracy. The God that Failed: Economics and Politics of Monarchy, Democracy and Natural Order (**Perspectives on Democratic Practice.** Routledge. 2001

Hoppe, Hans-Hermann: The Economics and Ethics of Private Property: Studies in Political Economy and Philosophy, 2nd Edition. Ludwig von Mises Institute. 2010

Hoppe, Hans-Herman: The Myth of National Defense: Essays on the Theory and History of Security Production. Ludwig von Mises Institute. 2003

Horwitz, Steve: Hayek's Modern Family: Classical Liberalism and the Evolution of Social Institutions. Palgrave Macmillan. 2015

Howden, David and Joseph T. Salerno (eds.): The Fed at One Hundred: A Critical View on the Federal Reserve System. Springer. 2014

Huebert, Jacob H.: Libertarianism Today. Praeger 2010

Huerta de Soto, Jesus: Money, Bank Credit, and Economic Cycles. Ludwig von Mises Institute. 2012

Hülsmann, Jörg Guido and Stephan Kinsella (eds.): Property, Freedom, and Society: Essays in Honor of Hans-Hermann Hoppe (LvMI). Ludwig von Mises Institute 2011

Hülsmann, Jörg Guido: The Ethics of Money Production. Ludwig von Mises Institute. 2008

Humboldt, Wilhelm von: The Sphere and Duties of Government (The Limits of State Action). Martino Fine Books. 2014

Illich, Ivan: Deschooling Society (Open Forum S). Marion Boyars Publishers Ltd; New edition edition. 2000

Illich, Ivan: Limits to Medicine: Medical Nemesis, the Expropriation of Health. Marion Boyars Publishers Ltd; Revised ed. Edition. 2000

Infantino, Lorenzo: Individualism in Modern Thought: From Adam Smith to Hayek (Routledge Studies in Social and Political Thought). Routledge 2014

Irwin, Douglas A.: Against the Tide. An Intellectual History of Free Trade. Princeton University Press. 1996

Joshi, Vijay: India's Long Road: The Search for Prosperity. Oxford University Press. 2017

Juma, Calestous: Innovation and Its Enemies: Why People Resist New Technologies. Oxford University Press. 2016

Kant, Imanuel and H.S. Reiss (ed). Kant: Political Writings (Cambridge Texts in the History of Political Thought). Cambridge University Press. 1991

Kealey, Terence: The Case Against Public Science. Cato Unbound. August 2013

Kealey, Terence: The Economic Laws of Scientific Research. Palgrave Macmillan. 1996

Kengor, Paul: The Politically Incorrect Guide to Communism (The Politically Incorrect Guides). Regnery Publishing 2017

Kenny, Charles: Getting Better: Why Global Development Is Succeeding – And How We Can Improve the World Even More. Basic Books. 2012

Keynes, John Maynard: The General Theory of Employment, Interest and Money: With the Economic Consequences of the Peace (Classics of World Literature). Wordworth Editions 2017

Kinsella, Stephan: Against Intellectual Property. Ludwig von Mises Institute. 2015

Kirzner, Israel: Competition and Entrepreneurship (The Collected Works of Israel M. Kirzner). Liberty Fund. 2013

Knight, Frank: Risk, Uncertainty and Profit. Martino Fine Books. 2014

Kocka, Jürgen: Capitalism. A Short History. Princeton University Press. 2017

Kroeber, Arthur A.: China's Economy: What Everyone Needs to Know. Oxford University Press. 2016

Kuehnelt-Leddihn: Eric Ritter von: Liberty or Equality: The Challenge of Our Times. The Ludwig von Mises Institute. 2014

Kuehnelt-Leddihn: Eric Ritter von: Menace of the Herd or Procrustes at Large. Ludwig von Mises Institute. 2012

Kurer, Oskar: John Stuart Mill (Routledge Revivals): The Politics of Progress. Routledge 2018
Kurer, Oskar: The Political Foundations of Development Policies. UPA Publishers 1996

Kurlansky, Mark: Nonviolence: The History of a Dangerous Idea (Modern Library Chronicles). Modern Library 2008

Kurzweil, Ray: The Singularity Is Near: When Humans Transcend Biology. Penguin Books. 2006

Lavoie, Don: Rivalry and Central Planning. The Socialist Calculation Debate Reconsidered (Advanced Studies in Political Economy). Mercatus Center at George Mason University. 2015

Leeson, Peter: Anarchy Unbound: Why Self-Governance Works Better Than You Think (Cambridge Studies in Economics, Choice, and Society). Cambridge University Press. 2014

Leonard, Thomas C.: Illiberal Reformers: Race, Eugenics, and American Economics in the Progressive Era. Princeton University Press. 2017

Legutko, Ryszard: The Demon in Democracy: Totalitarian Temptations in Free Societies. Encounter Books. 2016

Lenin, Vladimir Ilich: State and Revolution. Martino Fine Books. 2011

Leoni, Bruno: Freedom and the Law. **Liberty Fund. 1991**

Lerch, Hubert: An Introduction to Political Philosophy. **CreateSpace Independent Publishing Platform. 2011**

Levin, Mark R.: Rediscovering Americanism: And the Tyranny of Progressivism. **Threshold Editions. 2017**

Levitsky, Steven and Daniel Zieblatt: How Democracies Die. **Crown 2018**

Lewis, Hunter: Economics in Three Lessons and One Hundred Economics Laws: Two Works in One Volume. **Axios Press. 2017**

Lewis, Hunter: Where Keynes Went Wrong: And Why World Governments Keep Creating Inflation, Bubbles, and Busts. **Axios Press. 2009**

Lilla, Mark: The Once and Future Liberal: After Identity Politics. **Harper. 2017**

Lindsay, Brink: The Age of Abundance: How Prosperity Transformed America's Politics and Culture. **Harper Business Reprint edition. 2008**

Lingle, Christopher: The Rise and Decline of the Asian Century: False Starts on the Path to the Global Millennium. **Bookworld Services. 1998**

Lingle, Christopher: The Rise and Decline of the Asian Century: False Starts on the Path to the Global Millennium. **Bookworld Services. 1998**

Machaj, Mateusz: Money, Interest, and the Structure of Production: Resolving Some Puzzles in the Theory of Capital **(Capitalist Thought: Studies in Philosophy, Politics, and Economics). Lexington Books. 2017**

Mallaby, Sebastian: The Man Who Knew: The Life and Times of Alan Greenspan. **Penguin Books. 2017**

Maltsev, Yuri: Requiem for Marx. **CreateSpace Independent Publishing Platform. 1993**

Maltsev, Yuri: Mass Murder and Public Slavery: The Soviet Experience. **The Independent Review 2017**

Mandeville, Bernard: The Fable of the Bees and Other Writings **(Hackett Classics). Hacket Publishing Company. 1997**

Marx, Karl: Das Kapital: A Critique of Political Economy. **CreateSpace Independent Publishing Platform. 2011**

Marx, Karl and Friedrich Engels: The Communist Manifesto. **International Publishers Co; New edition. 2014**

McCaffrey, Matthew: The Economic Theory of Costs: Foundations and New Directions (Routledge Frontiers of Political Economy). Routledge 2017

McCloskey, Deirdre: The Bourgeois Virtues: Ethics for an Age of Commerce. University of Chicago Press. 2007

McGroarty, Emmett, Jane Robbins, and Erin Tuttle: Deconstructing the Administrative State. Liberty Hill Publishing. 2017

McLuhan, Marshall: The Gutenberg Galaxy. University of Toronto Press, Scholarly Publishing Division. 2011

Menger, Carl: Principles of Economics. CreateSpace Independent Publishing Platform. 2007

Mencken, H. L.: Notes on Democracy. CreateSpace Independent Publishing Platform. 2013

Mesquita, Bruce Bueno de and Alistair Smith: The Dictator's Handbook: Why Bad Behavior is Almost Always Good Politics. PublicAffairs. 2012

Mierzejewski, Alfred C.: Ludwig Erhard: A Biography. University of North Carolina Press. 2014

Mill, John Stuart: On Liberty, Utilitarianism and Other Essays (Oxford World's Classics). Cambridge University Press. 2015

Miller, Tom: China's Asian Dream: Empire Building along the New Silk Road. Zed Books. 2017

Mises, Ludwig von: Human Action. The Scholar's Edition. Ludwig von Mises Institute. 2010

Mises, Ludwig von: Liberalism. Liberty Fund. 2005

Mises, Ludwig von: Economic Calculation in the Socialist Commonwealth. Ludwig von Mises Institute. 2012

Mises, Ludwig von: Interventionism: An Economic Analysis (Lib Works Ludwig Von Mises PB). Liberty Fund. 2011

Mokyr, Joel: A Culture of Growth: The Origins of the Modern Economy (Graz Schumpeter Lectures). Princeton University Press 2016

Mokyr, Joel: Gift of Athena: Historical Origins of the Knowledge Economy. Princeton University Press 2014

Mokyr, Joel: The Lever of Riches: Technological Creativity and Economic Progress. Oxford University Press. 1992

Molyneux, Stefan: Practical Anarchy. The Freedom of the Future. CreateSpace Independent Publishing Platform. 2017

Mueller, Antony P.: Bubble or New Era? Monetary Aspects of the New Economy. In: Birner, Jack and Pierre Garrouste (eds): Markets, Information and Communication: Austrian Perspectives on the Internet Economy (Routledge Foundations of the Market Economy). Routledge. 2003, pp. 249-261

Muller, Jerry Z.: The Tyranny of Metrics. Princeton University Press. 2018

Muller, Jerry Z.: The Mind and the Market: Capitalism in Western Thought. Anchor. 2003

Murphy, Robert: The Politically Incorrect Guide to the Great Depression and the New Deal (The Politically Incorrect Guides). Regnery Publishing. 2009

Murphy, Robert: Choice: Cooperation, Enterprise, and Human Action. Independent Institute. 2015

Molinari, Gustave de: The Production of Security. Edited by Richard Ebeling with an Introduction by Murray Rothbard. Create Space. 2009

Murray, Charles: In Our Hands: A Plan to Replace the Welfare State. AEI Press. 2016

Murray, Charles: By the People: Rebuilding Liberty Without Permission. Crown Forum. 2015

Murray, Charles: Losing Ground: American Social Policy, 1950-1980. Basic Books. 2015

Nietzsche, Friedrich: The Will to Power. Independently published. 2017

Niskanen, William A.: Reaganomics: An Insider's Account of the Policies and the People. Oxford University Press. 1988

Norberg, Johan: Ten Reasons to Look Forward to the Future. Oneworld Publication. 2017

North, Douglas C. and Robert Paul Thomas: The Rise of the Western World: A New Economic History. Cambridge University Press. 1976

North, Douglass C.: Institutions, Institutional Change and Economic Performance (Political Economy of Institutions and Decisions) Cambridge University Press. 1990

North, Gary: Mises on Money. Ludwig von Mises Institute. 2012

Novak, Michael and Paul Adams: Social Justice Isn't What You Think It Is. Encounter Books. 2015

Nozick, Robert: Anarchy, State, and Utopia. Basic Books Reprint. 2013

O'Driscoll, Gerald P. and Maria Rizzo: The Economics of Time and Ignorance. Routledge Foundations of the Market Economy. Routledge 1996

OECD (Organization for Economic Cooperation and Development: The Sources of Economic Growth in OECD Countries. OECD 2003

Oliver, Michael J.: The New Libertarianism: Anarcho-Capitalism. CreateSpace. 2013

Olson, Mancur: The Logic of Collective Action. Public Goods and the Theory of Groups. Second printing with new preface and appendix (Harvard Economic Studies). Harvard University Press. 1971

Oppenheimer, Franz: The State: Its History and Development Viewed Sociologically. (Classic Reprint). Forgotten Books. 2012

O'Rourke, P. J.: Parliament of Whores: A Lone Humorist Attempts to Explain the Entire U.S. Government. Grove Press. 2003

O'Rourke, P. J.: Eat the Rich: A Treatise on Economics. Atlantic Monthly Press. 1999

Ortega y Gasset, José: The Revolt of the Masses. W. W. Norten & Company. 1994

Ostrom, Elinor: Governing the Commons: The Evolution of Institutions for Collective Action (Canto Classics). Cambridge University Press; Reissue edition. 2015

Ostrowski, James: Progressivism: A Primer on the Idea Destroying America. Cazenovia Books. 2014

Palmer, Tom: Realizing Freedom: Libertarian Theory, History, and Practice. Cato Institute. 2014

Palmer, Tom G, Virginia Prostel, Brink Lindsey, and Tyler Cowen: Libertarianism. Past and Prospects (Cato Unbound Book 32007). Cato Institute. 2007

Parijs, Philippe Van and Yannick Vanderborght: Basic Income: A Radical Proposal for a Free Society and a Sane Economy. Harvard University Press. 2017

Paul, Ron: End the Fed. Grand Central Publishing. 2010

Paul, Ron: Revolution. A Manifesto. Grand Central Publishing. 2009

Pesek, William: Japanization: What the World Can Learn from Japan's Lost Decades. Wiley 2014

Pilling, David: The Growth Delusion: Wealth, Poverty, and the Well-Being of Nations. Tim Duggan Books. 2018

Pinker, Steven: Enlightenment Now: The Case for Reason, Science, Humanism, and Progress. Viking 2018

Pinker, Steven: The Better Angels of Our Nature: Why Violence Has Declined. Penguin Books. 2012

Postrel, Virginia: The Future and Its Enemies: The Growing Conflict Over Creativity, Enterprise. Free Press. 2011

Powell, Benjamin: Out of Poverty: Sweatshops in the Global Economy (Cambridge Studies in Economics, Choice, and Society). Cambridge University Press. 2014

Powell, Jim: FDR's Folly: How Roosevelt and His New Deal Prolonged the Great Depression. Crown Forum. 2004

Powell, James and Paul Johnson: The Triumph of Liberty: A 2,000 Year History Told Through the Lives of Freedom's Greatest Champions. Free Press. 2000

Qui, Insula: Capitalism Works. Independently published. 2018

Rachels, Chase and Christopher Chase Rachels: A Spontaneous Order: The Capitalist Case for a Stateless Society. CreateSpace Independent Publishing Platform. 2015

Raico, Ralph: Classical Liberalism and the Austrian School. CreateSpace Independent Publishing Platform. 2012

Raico, Ralph: Great Wars and Great Leaders: A Libertarian Rebuttal. Ludwig von Mises Institute. 2015

Ratner-Rosenhagen, Jennifer: American Nietzsche: A History of an Icon and His Ideas. University of Chicago Press; Reprint edition. 2012

Rawls, John: Justice as Fairness: A Restatement. Belknap Press: An Imprint of Harvard University Press. 2001

Rand, Ayn: Capitalism. The Unknown Ideal. Signet; Reissue edition. 1986

Reed, Lawrence R.: Great Myth of the Great Depression. Foundation for Economic Education. 2015

Reisman, George: Capitalism. A Treatise on Economics. TJS Books 1996

Reisman, George: The Government Against the Economy. Jameson Books. 1985

Reybrouck, David van: Against Elections. The Case for Democracy. Random House U.K. 2017

Reynolds, Morgan O.: Making America Poorer: The Cost of Labor Law. Cato Institute. 1987

Richman, Sheldon: America's Counter-Revolution: The Constitution Revisited. Grifien & Lash. 2016

Ridley, Matt: The Rational Optimist: How Prosperity Evolves. Harper Perennial. 2011

Rifkin, Jeremy: The Zero Marginal Cost Society: The Internet of Things, the Collaborative Commons, and the Eclipse of Capitalism. St. Martin's Griffin; Reprint edition. 2015

Ritenour, Shawn (ed.): The Mises Reader Unabridged. Ludwig von Mises Institute. 2016

Roberts, Paul Craig: The Tyranny of Good Intentions: How Prosecutors and Law Enforcement Are Trampling the Constitution in the Name of Justice. Crown. 2008

Rockwell, Llewellyn, H. Jr.: Against the State. An Anarcho-Capitalist Manifesto. Rockwell Communication. 2014

Rosenberg, Nathan and L. E. Birdzell: How the West Grew Rich: The Economic Transformation Of The Industrial World. Basic Books. 1987

Rosling, Hans, Anna Rosling Rönnlund, Ola Rosling: Factfulness: Ten Reasons We're Wrong About the World--and Why Things Are Better Than You Think. Flatiron Books 2018

Rothbard, Murray N.: Anatomy of the State. Bhpublishing. 2014

Rothbard, Murray N.: For a New Liberty. The Libertarian Manifesto. CreateSpace Independent Publishing Platform. 2006

Rothbard, Murray N.: What Has Government Done to Our Money? Ludwig von Mises Institute. 2015

Rothbard, Murray N.: Man, Economy, and State with Power and Market, Scholar's Edition. Ludwig von Mises Institute. 2011
Rothbard, Murray N.: America's Great Depression. Ludwig von Mises Institute. 2000
Rummel, Rudy J.: Death by Government: Genocide and Mass Murder Since 1900. Routledge 1997

Rummel, Rudy J.: The Blue Book of Freedom: Ending Famine, Poverty, Democide, and War. Cumberland House Publishing. 2007

Salerno, Joseph T.: Money: Sound and Unsound. Ludwig von Mises Institute. 2015

Say, Jean-Baptiste: A Treatise on Political Economy: Or the Production, Distribution and Consumption of Wealth. CreateSpace Independent Publishing Platform. 2013

Schiff, Peter: How an Economy Grows and Why It Crashes. Wiley. 2010

Schmitt, Carl: The Leviathan in the State Theory of Thomas Hobbes: Meaning and Failure of a Political Symbol (Heritage of Sociology). University of Chicago Press Ed Edition. 2008

Schmitt, Carl: The Concept of the Political: Expanded Edition Enlarged Edition with a Commentary by Leo Strauss. The University of Chicago Press. 2007

Schoolland, Ken: The Adventures of Jonathan Gullible. A Free Market Odyssey. Liberty Publishing. 2011

Schumpeter, Joseph A.: Business Cycles: A Theoretical, Historical, and Statistical Analysis of the Capitalist Process (2 Vols.). Martino Fine Books. 2017

Schumpeter, Joseph A.: Can Capitalism Survive?: Creative Destruction and the Future of the Global Economy. Harper Perennial Modern Classics. 2009

Schumpeter, Joseph A.: Capitalism, Socialism, and Democracy: Third Edition. Harper Perennial Modern Classics. 2008

Schumpeter, Joseph A.: Essays: On Entrepreneurs, Innovations, Business Cycles and the Evolution of Capitalism. Routledge 1989

Schumpeter, Joseph A.: Theory of Economic Development (Social Science Classics Series). Routledge 1981

Schwab, Klaus and Nicholas Davis, Satya Nadella: Shaping the Fourth Industrial Revolution. World Economic Forum. 2018

Scruton, Roger: Fools, Frauds and Firebrands: Thinkers of the New Left. Bloomsbury Continuum. 2017

Selgin, George: Financial Stability without Central Banks. London Publishing Partnership. 2018

Selgin, George: Money: Free and Unfree. Cato Institute. 2017

Selgin, George: Less Than Zero. The Case for a Falling Price Level in a Growing Economy. CreateSpace Independent Publishing Platform. 2014

Selgin, George: The Theory of Free Banking. Rowman & Littlefield Publisher. 1988

Sen, Amartya: Development as Freedom. Anchor. 2000

Sévillia, Jean: Le terrorisme intellectuel (French Edition). Tempus Perrain. 2017

Shaffer, Butler: Boundaries of Order: Private Property as a Social System. CreateSpace Independent Publishing Platform. 2009

Shaffer, Buttler: The Wizards of Ozymandias: Reflections on the Decline and Fall. CreateSpace Independent Publishing Platform. 2012

Shlae, Amity: The Forgotten Man: A New History of the Great Depression Harper Perennial. 2008

Simon, Julian Lincoln: The Ultimate Resource 2. Princeton University Press. 1998

Sintomer, Yves: Das demokratische Experiment: Geschichte des Losverfahrens in der Politik von Athen bis heute (German Edition). Springer 2016

Smiley, Gene: Rethinking the Great Depression (American Ways). Ivan R. Dee Publisher. 2003

Smith, Adam: The Theory of Moral Sentiments. Digireads.com. 2010

Smith, Adam: The Wealth of Nations (Bantam Classics). Bantam Classics; Annotated edition. 2003

Snyder, Timothy: On Tyranny: Twenty Lessons from the Twentieth Century. Tim Duggan Books. 2017

Sombart, Werner: The Quintessence Of Capitalism: A Study Of The History And Psychology Of The Modern Business Man. Scholar Select. Andesite Press. 2017

Solzhenitsyn, Aleksandr: The Gulag Archipelago. The Harvill Press. 2003

Soto, Hernando de: The Mystery of Capital: Why Capitalism Triumphs in the West and Fails Everywhere Else. Basic Books. 2003

Sowell, Thomas: Basic Economics. Basic Books. 2014

Sowell, Thomas: Economic Facts and Fallacies. Basic Books. 2011

Sowell, Thomas: The Quest for Cosmic Justice. Free Press 2002

Spencer, Herbert: Social Statics: Or, The Conditions Essential to Human Happiness Specified and the First of them Developed. Nabu Press. 2011

Srinivasa, Bhu: Americana: A 400-Year History of American Capitalism. Penguin Press. 2017

Steil, Ben: The Marshall Plan: Dawn of the Cold War. Simon & Schuster. 2018

Steil, Ben: The Battle of Bretton Woods: John Maynard Keynes, Harry Dexter White, and the Making of a New World Order (Council on Foreign Relations Books). Princeton University Press. 2014

Stirner, Max: The Ego and His Own: The Case of the Individual Against Authority (Dover Books on Western Philosophy). Dover Publications. 2005

Stone, Peter: Lotteries in Public Life: A Reader (Sortition and Public Policy). Imprint Academic. 2012

Stringham, Edward Peter: Private Governance: Creating Order in Economic and Social Life. Oxford University Press. 2015

Susskind, Richard and Daniel Susskind: The Future of the Professions: How Technology Will Transform the Work of Human Experts. Oxford University Press. Reprint edition. 2017

Suvorov, Viktor: Icebreaker. Who Started the Second World War? PL UK Publishing. 2012

Taleb, Nassim Nicholas: Skin in the Game: Hidden Asymmetries in Daily Life. Random House 2018

Taylor, Frederick: The Downfall of Money: Germany's Hyperinflation and the Destruction of the Middle Class. Bloomsbury Press. 2015

Taylor, Mark Zachary: The Politics of Innovation: Why Some Countries Are Better Than Others at Science and Technology. Oxford University Press. 2016

Thiel, Peter: Zero to One: Notes on Startups, or How to Build the Future. Currency Publishers. 2014

Thornton, Mark: The Bastiat Collection. Ludwig von Mises Institute. 2017

Thornton, Mark: The Economics of Prohibition. Ludwig von Mises Institute. 2014

Tilly, Charles: Coercion, Capital and European States, A.D. 990 – 1992. Wiley-Blackwell. 1992

Tirole, Jean: Economics for the Common Good. Princeton University Press. 2017

Tooley, Hunt: The Great War: Western Front and Home Front. Palgrave 2015

Tucker, Jeffrey: A Beautiful Anarchy: How to Create Your Own Civilization in the Digital Age. Laissez Faire Books. 2012

Vance, Laurence M.: War, Empire, and the Military: Essays on the Follies of War and U.S. Foreign Policy. Vance Publications. 2014

Vedder, Richard: Going Broke By Degree: Why College Cost. AEI Press. 2004

Veryser, Harry C.: It Didn't Have to Be This Way: Why Boom and Bust Is Unnecessary—and How the Austrian School of Economics Breaks the Cycle (Culture of Enterprise). ISI Books. 2013

Volcker, Paul and Toyoo Gyohten. Changing Fortunes. Crown. 1992

Walsh, Michael: The Devil's Pleasure Palace: The Cult of Critical Theory and the Subversion of the West. Encounter Books. 2017

White, Lawrence: The Clash of Economic Ideas: The Great Policy Debates and Experiments of the Last Hundred Years. Cambridge University Press. 2012

White, Lawrence: The Theory of Monetary Institutions. Wiley-Blackwell. 1999

White, Lawrence: Competition and Currency: Essays on Free Banking and Money. New York University Press. 1992

Wisniewski, Jakub: The Economics of Law, Order, and Action: The Logic of Public Goods (Routledge Advances in Heterodox Economics). Routledge. 2018

Williams, Walter E.: American Contempt for Liberty (Hoover Institution Press Publication). Hoover Institution Press 2015

Williams, Walter E.: Race & Economics: How Much Can Be Blamed on Discrimination?. Hoover Institution Press. 2011

Wolfram, Gary: A Capitalist Manifesto: Understanding The Market Economy And Defending Liberty. Dunlap Goddard. 2013

Woods, Thomas E.: Meltdown: A Free-Market Look at Why the Stock Market Collapsed, the Economy Tanked, and Government Bailouts Will Make Things Worse. Regnery 2009

Yergin, Daniel and Joseph Stanislaw: The Commanding Heights: The Battle for the World Economy. Free Press. 2002

Zelmanovitz, Leonidas: The Ontology and Function of Money: The Philosophical Fundamentals of Monetary Institutions (Capitalist Thought: Studies in Philosophy, Politics, and Economics). Lexington Books 2015

Antony P. Mueller

ABOUT THE AUTHOR

Antony P. Mueller is a German professor of economics who currently teaches at the Federal University UFS in Brazil where he also serves in the graduate and doctoral programs in economics and sociology. He holds a doctorate in economics from the Friedrich-Alexander University Erlangen-Nuremberg, Germany.

Contact:
antonymueller@gmx.com
See his Amazon author page:https://www.amazon.com/ANTONY-P.-MUELLER/e/B07BHF4RG8/ref=ntt_dp_epwbk_0

Related publications
"How Capitalism creates wealth and promotes prosperity" is based on the monograph "Beyond the State and Politics", which also includes parts about Socialism, Interventionism, the Welfare State, and Economic Policy.

www.ingramcontent.com/pod-product-compliance
Lightning Source LLC
Chambersburg PA
CBHW031418210526
45464CB00005B/1938